Children and Social Work Act 2017

CHAPTER 16

Explanatory Notes are available separately

GRANGIS UK Publishing

Adapted and published by GRANGIS (Grand Register Library).
Online: www.grangis.com
E-mail: contact@grangis.com

© Crown Copyright
Contains public sector information licensed under the Open Government Licence v3.0.
You may re-use this publication free of charge in any format or medium. You must re-use it accurately and not in a misleading context.

© GRANGIS 2022.
In this version:
ISBN: 979-8-88559-011-2
Where we have identified any copyrighted material, you will need to obtain written permission for re-use.
Note: This is the original version (as it was originally enacted). Title, sub-title and the generated date is as marked on the page.

Children and Social Work Act 2017

CHAPTER 16

CHILDREN AND SOCIAL WORK ACT 2017

PART 1

CHILDREN

CHAPTER 1

LOOKED AFTER CHILDREN

Corporate parenting principles for English local authorities

1 Corporate parenting principles

Care leavers in England

2 Local offer for care leavers
3 Advice and support

Educational achievement in England

4 Duty of local authority in relation to previously looked after children
5 Maintained schools: staff member for previously looked after pupils
6 Academies: staff member for looked after and previously looked after pupils
7 Maintained schools: guidance for staff member for looked after pupils

Care and adoption proceedings in England and Wales

8 Care orders: permanence provisions
9 Adoption: duty to have regard to relationship with adopters

Secure accommodation

10　Placing children in secure accommodation elsewhere in Great Britain

Chapter 1: consequential amendments

11　Chapter 1: consequential amendments

CHAPTER 2

SAFEGUARDING OF CHILDREN

Child Safeguarding Practice Review Panel

12　Child Safeguarding Practice Review Panel
13　Functions of the Panel
14　Events to be notified to the Panel
15　Information

Local arrangements for safeguarding and promoting welfare of children

16　Local arrangements for safeguarding and promoting welfare of children
17　Local child safeguarding practice reviews
18　Further provision about arrangements
19　Information
20　Funding
21　Combining safeguarding partner areas and delegating functions
22　Guidance by Secretary of State
23　Interpretation

Child death reviews

24　Child death reviews
25　Information
26　Funding
27　Combining child death review partner areas and delegating functions
28　Guidance and interpretation

Miscellaneous

29　Regulations under provisions inserted by sections 13, 16 and 17
30　Abolition of Local Safeguarding Children Boards
31　Chapter 2: consequential amendments

CHAPTER 3

OTHER PROVISION RELATING TO CHILDREN'S SOCIAL CARE

Children's social care: pre-employment protection of whistle-blowers

32　Pre-employment protection of whistle-blowers

Combined authority functions relating to children

33　Power to secure proper performance

CHAPTER 4

RELATIONSHIPS, SEX AND PSHE EDUCATION

34 Education relating to relationships and sex
35 Other personal, social, health and economic education

PART 2

SOCIAL WORKERS ETC IN ENGLAND

Social Work England

36 Social Work England
37 Over-arching objective
38 Advisers

Regulation and improvement

39 Registration
40 Restrictions on practice and protected titles
41 Professional standards
42 Improvement standards
43 Education and training
44 Discipline and fitness to practise
45 Offences

Provision of training

46 Ensuring adequate provision of social work training
47 Exercise by Special Health Authority of functions under section 46(1)(b)

Approval of courses in relation to mental health professionals

48 Approval of courses for approved mental health professionals
49 Approval of courses for best interests assessors

Fees and grants

50 Fees
51 Grants

Information and co-operation

52 Information and advice
53 Duty to co-operate

Oversight

54 Information for Secretary of State
55 Default powers
56 Oversight by the Professional Standards Authority for Health and Social Care

Regulations under Part 2

57 Conferral of functions and sub-delegation

58 Consultation
59 Parliamentary procedure for regulations under Part 2

Transfer scheme and consequential amendments

60 Transfer scheme
61 Repeal of existing powers to regulate social workers
62 Amendments to do with this Part

Interpretation

63 Interpretation of Part 2

Review

64 Review by independent person

PART 3

GENERAL

65 Power to make transitional provision
66 Power to make consequential provision
67 Regulations: general
68 Affirmative and negative resolution procedures
69 Extent
70 Commencement
71 Short title

SCHEDULES

SCHEDULE 1 — Placing children in secure accommodation elsewhere in Great Britain
1 Children Act 1989
2 (1) Section 25 (use of accommodation in England for restricting...
3 In paragraph 19(9) of Schedule 2 (restrictions on arrangements for...
4 Children (Secure Accommodation) Regulations 1991 (S.I. 1991/1505)
5 In regulation 1— (a) in the heading, for "and commencement"...
6 In regulation 2(1) (interpretation), in the definition of "children's home",...
7 For regulation 3 substitute— Approval by Secretary of State of...
8 In regulation 17 (records), in the words before paragraph (a),...
9 Secure Accommodation (Scotland) Regulations 2013 (S.S.I. 2013 No. 205)
10 In regulation 5 (maximum period in secure accommodation), after paragraph...
11 In regulation 15 (records to be kept by managers of...
12 Children's Hearings (Scotland) Act 2011 (Consequential and Transitional Provisions and Savings) Order 2013 (S.I. 2013 No. 1465)
13 Social Services and Well-being (Wales) Act 2014 (anaw 4)
14 Saving for existing powers

SCHEDULE 2 — Part 1 of this Act: consequential amendments
   Part 1 — AMENDMENT RELATING TO CHAPTER 1

1 Local offer for care leavers
2 In paragraph 1(2)(a) of Schedule 2 to the Children Act...
3 In section 135(1)(e) of the Education and Inspections Act 2006...
4 In section 30 of the Children and Families Act 2014...
5 Advice and support
6 In section 83A(5)(a) of the Apprenticeships, Skills, Children and Learning...

Part 2 — AMENDMENTS RELATING TO ABOLITION OF LOCAL SAFEGUARDING CHILDREN BOARDS

7 In Schedule 1 to the Local Authority Social Services Act...
8 (1) Section 83 of the Children Act 1989 (research and...
9 (1) Section 31 of the Children and Young Persons Act...

SCHEDULE 3 — Social Work England

1 Status
2 Members
3 Term of office
4 A member may resign by giving written notice to the...
5 The Secretary of State may by notice in writing remove...
6 Remuneration and pensions
7 If required to do so by the Secretary of State,...
8 Staff
9 The regulator may appoint other staff.
10 (1) The regulator's staff may be appointed on such terms,...
11 Procedure
12 No proceeding is invalidated by— (a) a vacancy in the...
13 Delegation
14 (1) The regulator may delegate functions to any other person...
15 (1) A function may be delegated under paragraph 13 or...
16 Membership of committees and sub-committees
17 Annual reports and accounts
18 (1) The regulator must keep proper accounts and proper records...
19 The Secretary of State must, in respect of each financial...
20 In paragraphs 17 to 19 "financial year" means—
21 Application of seal and evidence
22 A document purporting to be duly executed under the seal...
23 Disqualification
24 Freedom of information

SCHEDULE 4 — Oversight by the Professional Standards Authority for Health and Social Care

1 The National Health Service Reform and Health Care Professions Act...
2 (1) Section 25 (the Professional Standards Authority for Health and...
3 (1) Section 25A (funding of the Authority) is amended as...
4 After section 25A insert— Funding of the Authority by Social...
5 In section 25C (appointments to regulatory bodies), in subsection (7),...
6 (1) Section 25D (power of regulatory bodies to establish voluntary...
7 In section 25E (section 25D: interpretation), omit subsections (10) and...
8 In section 25F (establishment of voluntary register: impact assessment), in...
9 In section 25G (power of the Authority to accredit voluntary...
10 In section 25H (accreditation of voluntary register: impact assessment), in...

11	In section 25I (functions of the Authority in relation to...
12	(1) Section 26A (powers of Secretary of State and devolved...
13	In section 27 (regulatory bodies and the Authority), in subsection...
14	In section 28 (complaints), in subsection (1), after "regulatory body"...
15	(1) Section 29 (reference to disciplinary cases by the Authority...
16	(1) Section 38 (regulations and orders) is amended as follows....

SCHEDULE 5 — Amendments to do with Part 2
Part 1 — GENERAL AMENDMENTS

1	London County Council (General Powers) Act 1920
2	Medicines Act 1968
3	Video Recordings Act 1984
4	London Local Authorities Act 1991
5	Value Added Tax Act 1994
6	Data Protection Act 1998
7	Care Standards Act 2000
8	(1) Section 55 is amended as follows.
9	(1) Section 67 is amended as follows.
10	Health and Social Work Professions Order 2001
11	(1) Article 3 is amended as follows.
12	In article 6(3)(aa), omit "or social work".
13	In article 7(4), omit "or social work".
14	(1) Article 9 is amended as follows.
15	(1) Article 10 is amended as follows.
16	In article 11A, omit paragraph (11).
17	(1) Article 12 is amended as follows.
18	(1) Article 13 is amended as follows.
19	For the heading of article 13A substitute "Visiting health professionals...
20	Omit article 13B.
21	In article 19(2A)(b), omit "or social work".
22	In article 20, omit the words from "; but the...
23	(1) Article 37 is amended as follows.
24	(1) Article 38 is amended as follows.
25	In article 39, omit paragraph (1A).
26	In Schedule 1, in paragraph 1A(1)(b), omit paragraph (ia) (but...
27	(1) In Schedule 3, paragraph 1 is amended as follows....
28	Adoption and Children Act 2002
29	Income Tax (Earnings and Pensions) Act 2003
30	National Health Service Act 2006
31	National Health Service (Wales) Act 2006
32	Armed Forces Act 2006
33	Safeguarding Vulnerable Groups Act 2006
34	In section 41(7), in the table, after entry 10 insert—...
35	In Schedule 3, in paragraph 16(4), after paragraph (l) insert—...
36	Protection of Vulnerable Groups (Scotland) Act 2007 (asp 14)
37	Children and Young Persons Act 2008
38	Health and Social Care Act 2012
39	Regulation and Inspection of Social Care (Wales) Act 2016 (anaw 2)
40	In section 111(4)(b)— (a) in the Welsh text, for "Cyngor...
41	In section 117(4)(a)— (a) in the Welsh text, after "Gofal"...
42	In section 119(4)(a)(ii)— (a) in the Welsh text, for "y...
43	In section 125(5)(a)(ii)— (a) in the Welsh text, for "y...
44	In section 174(5)(a)(ii)— (a) in the Welsh text, for "Cyngor...

Part 2 — RENAMING OF HEALTH AND SOCIAL WORK PROFESSIONS ORDER 2001
45 For the title to the Health and Social Work Professions...
46 In article 1(1) of that Order (citation), for "the Health...
47 In the following provisions, for "the Health and Social Work...
48 In the definition of "registered psychologist" in each of the...

Children and Social Work Act 2017

2017 CHAPTER 16

An Act to make provision about looked after children; to make other provision in relation to the welfare of children; and to make provision about the regulation of social workers. [27th April 2017]

BE IT ENACTED by the Queen's most Excellent Majesty, by and with the advice and consent of the Lords Spiritual and Temporal, and Commons, in this present Parliament assembled, and by the authority of the same, as follows:—

PART 1

CHILDREN

CHAPTER 1

LOOKED AFTER CHILDREN

Corporate parenting principles for English local authorities

1 Corporate parenting principles

(1) A local authority in England must, in carrying out functions in relation to the children and young people mentioned in subsection (2), have regard to the need—
   (a) to act in the best interests, and promote the physical and mental health and well-being, of those children and young people;
   (b) to encourage those children and young people to express their views, wishes and feelings;
   (c) to take into account the views, wishes and feelings of those children and young people;

(d) to help those children and young people gain access to, and make the best use of, services provided by the local authority and its relevant partners;

(e) to promote high aspirations, and seek to secure the best outcomes, for those children and young people;

(f) for those children and young people to be safe, and for stability in their home lives, relationships and education or work;

(g) to prepare those children and young people for adulthood and independent living.

(2) The children and young people mentioned in this subsection are—

(a) children who are looked after by a local authority, within the meaning given by section 22(1) of the Children Act 1989;

(b) relevant children within the meaning given by section 23A(2) of that Act;

(c) persons aged under 25 who are former relevant children within the meaning given by section 23C(1) of that Act.

(3) In this section—

"local authority in England" means—

(a) a county council in England;

(b) a district council;

(c) a London borough council;

(d) the Common Council of the City of London (in their capacity as a local authority);

(e) the Council of the Isles of Scilly;

(f) a combined authority established under section 103 of the Local Democracy, Economic Development and Construction Act 2009;

"relevant partners", in relation to a local authority, has the meaning given by section 10(4) of the Children Act 2004.

(4) A local authority in England must have regard to any guidance given by the Secretary of State as to the performance of the duty under subsection (1).

Care leavers in England

2 Local offer for care leavers

(1) A local authority in England must publish information about—

(a) services which the local authority offers for care leavers as a result of its functions under the Children Act 1989;

(b) other services which the local authority offers that may assist care leavers in, or in preparing for, adulthood and independent living.

(2) For the purposes of subsection (1), services which may assist care leavers in, or in preparing for, adulthood and independent living include services relating to—

(a) health and well-being;

(b) relationships;

(c) education and training;

(d) employment;

(e) accommodation;

(f) participation in society.

(3) Where it considers appropriate, a local authority in England must publish information about services for care leavers offered by others which the local authority has power to offer as a result of its functions under the Children Act 1989.

(4) Information required to be published by a local authority under this section is to be known as its "local offer for care leavers".

(5) A local authority must update its local offer for care leavers from time to time, as appropriate.

(6) Before publishing its local offer for care leavers (or any updated version) a local authority must consult relevant persons about which of the services offered by the local authority may assist care leavers in, or in preparing for, adulthood and independent living.

(7) In this section—

"care leavers" means—
  (a) eligible children within the meaning given by paragraph 19B of Schedule 2 to the Children Act 1989;
  (b) relevant children within the meaning given by section 23A(2) of that Act;
  (c) persons aged under 25 who are former relevant children within the meaning given by section 23C(1) of that Act;
  (d) persons qualifying for advice and assistance within the meaning given by section 24 of that Act;

"local authority in England" means—
  (a) a county council in England;
  (b) a district council;
  (c) a London borough council;
  (d) the Common Council of the City of London (in their capacity as a local authority);
  (e) the Council of the Isles of Scilly;
  (f) a combined authority established under section 103 of the Local Democracy, Economic Development and Construction Act 2009;

"relevant persons", in relation to a local authority, means such care leavers and other persons as appear to the local authority to be representative of care leavers in its area.

3   Advice and support

(1) The Children Act 1989 is amended as follows.

(2) After section 23CZA insert—

"23CZB England: further advice and support

(1) This section applies to a former relevant child if—
  (a) he or she has reached the age of 21 but not the age of 25, and
  (b) a local authority in England had duties towards him or her under section 23C (whether or not some of those duties continue to subsist by virtue of subsection (7) of that section).

(2) If the former relevant child informs the local authority that he or she wishes to receive advice and support under this section, the local authority has the duties provided for in subsections (3) to (6).

(3) The local authority must provide the former relevant child with a personal adviser until the former relevant child—

    (a) reaches the age of 25, or

    (b) if earlier, informs the local authority that he or she no longer wants a personal adviser.

(4) The local authority must—

    (a) carry out an assessment in relation to the former relevant child under subsection (5), and

    (b) prepare a pathway plan for the former relevant child.

(5) An assessment under this subsection is an assessment of the needs of the former relevant child with a view to determining—

    (a) whether any services offered by the local authority (under this Act or otherwise) may assist in meeting his or her needs, and

    (b) if so, what advice and support it would be appropriate for the local authority to provide for the purpose of helping the former relevant child to obtain those services.

(6) The local authority must provide the former relevant child with advice and support that it would be appropriate to provide as mentioned in subsection (5)(b).

(7) Where a former relevant child to whom this section applies is not receiving advice and support under this section, the local authority must offer such advice and support—

    (a) as soon as possible after he or she reaches the age of 21, and

    (b) at least once in every 12 months.

(8) In this section "former relevant child" has the meaning given by section 23C(1)."

(3) In section 23CA (further assistance to pursue education or training) for subsection (2) substitute—

"(2) It is the duty of the responsible local authority to provide a personal adviser for a person to whom this section applies."

(4) In section 23D (personal advisers) after subsection (2) insert—

"(3) Where a local authority in England ceases to be under a duty to provide a personal adviser for a person under any provision of this Part, that does not affect any other duty under this Part to provide a personal adviser for the person.

(4) Where a local authority in England has more than one duty under this Part to provide a personal adviser for a person, each duty is discharged by the provision of the same personal adviser (the local authority are not required to provide more than one personal adviser for the person)."

(5) Section 23E (pathway plans) is amended as follows.

(6) In subsection (1) (contents of pathway plan), after paragraph (a) (but before the "and" at the end) insert—

"(aa) in the case of a plan prepared under section 23CZB, the advice and support that the local authority intend to provide;".

(7) After subsection (1) insert—

"(1ZA) A local authority may carry out an assessment under section 23CZB(5) of a person's needs at the same time as any assessment of the person's needs is made under section 23CA(3)."

(8) In subsection (1A) (statutory assessments that may be carried out at the same time as assessment relating to a pathway plan) after "23B(3)" insert ", 23CZB(5)".

(9) In subsection (1B) (regulations about assessments) after "23B(3)" insert ", 23CZB(5)".

(10) In subsection (1D) (pathway plans to be kept under review) after "23B" insert ", 23CZB".

Educational achievement in England

4   Duty of local authority in relation to previously looked after children

Before section 23ZA of the Children Act 1989 (and the italic heading before it) insert—

"Educational achievement of previously looked after children

23ZZA Information and advice for promoting educational achievement

(1) A local authority in England must make advice and information available in accordance with this section for the purpose of promoting the educational achievement of each relevant child educated in their area.

(2) The advice and information must be made available to—
    (a) any person who has parental responsibility for the child,
    (b) the member of staff at the child's school designated under section 20A of the Children and Young Persons Act 2008 or by virtue of section 2E of the Academies Act 2010, and
    (c) any other person that the local authority consider appropriate.

(3) A local authority in England may do anything else that they consider appropriate with a view to promoting the educational achievement of relevant children educated in their area.

(4) A local authority in England must appoint at least one person for the purpose of discharging the duty imposed by subsection (1).

(5) The person appointed for that purpose must be an officer employed by the authority or another local authority in England.

(6) In this section—

"relevant child" means—
(a) a child who was looked after by the local authority or another local authority in England or Wales but ceased to be so looked after as a result of—
    (i) a child arrangements order which includes arrangements relating to with whom the child is to live, or when the child is to live with any person,
    (ii) a special guardianship order, or
    (iii) an adoption order within the meaning given by section 72(1) of the Adoption Act 1976 or section 46(1) of the Adoption and Children Act 2002, or
(b) a child who appears to the local authority—
    (i) to have been in state care in a place outside England and Wales because he or she would not otherwise have been cared for adequately, and
    (ii) to have ceased to be in that state care as a result of being adopted.

(7) For the purposes of this section a child is educated in a local authority's area if—
    (a) the child is receiving early years provision secured by the local authority under section 7(1) of the Childcare Act 2006, or
    (b) the child is of compulsory school age and—
        (i) the child attends a school in the local authority's area, or
        (ii) if the child does not attend school, the child receives all or most of his or her education in the local authority's area.

(8) For the purposes of this section a child is in "state care" if he or she is in the care of, or accommodated by—
    (a) a public authority,
    (b) a religious organisation, or
    (c) any other organisation the sole or main purpose of which is to benefit society."

5 Maintained schools: staff member for previously looked after pupils

After section 20 of the Children and Young Persons Act 2008 insert—

"20A Designated staff member for previously looked after pupils

(1) The governing body of a maintained school in England must—
    (a) designate a member of the staff at the school (the "designated person") as having responsibility for promoting the educational achievement of registered pupils within subsection (2), and
    (b) ensure that the designated person undertakes appropriate training and has regard to any guidance issued by the Secretary of State.

(2) A registered pupil is within this subsection if the pupil—
    (a) was looked after by a local authority but ceased to be looked after by them as a result of—

(i) a child arrangements order (within the meaning given by section 8(1) of the 1989 Act) which includes arrangements relating to with whom the child is to live, or when the child is to live with any person,

(ii) a special guardianship order (within the meaning given by section 14A(1) of the 1989 Act), or

(iii) an adoption order (within the meaning given by section 72(1) of the Adoption Act 1976 or section 46(1) of the Adoption and Children Act 2002), or

(b) appears to the governing body—

(i) to have been in state care in a place outside England and Wales because he or she would not otherwise have been cared for adequately, and

(ii) to have ceased to be in that state care as a result of being adopted.

(3) The Secretary of State may by regulations require the governing body of a maintained school in England to ensure that the designated person has qualifications or experience (or both) prescribed by the regulations.

(4) In exercising its functions under this section the governing body of a maintained school in England must have regard to any guidance issued by the Secretary of State.

(5) For the purposes of this section a person is "looked after by a local authority" if the person is looked after by a local authority for the purposes of the 1989 Act or Part 6 of the 2014 Act.

(6) For the purposes of this section a person is in "state care" if he or she is in the care of, or accommodated by—

(a) a public authority,

(b) a religious organisation, or

(c) any other organisation the sole or main purpose of which is to benefit society.

(7) In this section—

"maintained school" has the meaning given by section 39(1) of the Education Act 2002;

"registered pupil" has the meaning given by section 434(5) of the Education Act 1996."

6 Academies: staff member for looked after and previously looked after pupils

(1) After section 2D of the Academies Act 2010 insert—

"2E Provision about staff member for looked after and previously looked after pupils

(1) An Academy agreement must include provision requiring the proprietor of the Academy—

(a) to designate a member of staff at the Academy (the "designated person") as having responsibility for promoting the educational achievement of relevant pupils at the Academy,

(b) to ensure that the designated person undertakes appropriate training and has regard to any guidance issued by the Secretary of State, and

(c) in complying with provision included in the agreement by virtue of paragraph (a) or (b), to have regard to any guidance issued by the Secretary of State.

(2) An Academy agreement made before the day on which section 6 of the Children and Social Work Act 2017 (which inserts this section) comes fully into force is to be treated as if it included the provision required by subsection (1).

(3) The Secretary of State may by regulations—

(a) require an Academy agreement to include provision requiring the proprietor of the Academy—

(i) to ensure that a designated person has qualifications or experience (or both) prescribed by the regulations, and

(ii) in complying with provision included in the agreement by virtue of sub-paragraph (i), to have regard to any guidance issued by the Secretary of State;

(b) provide that an Academy agreement made before the day on which the regulations come into force is to be treated as if it included any provision required under paragraph (a).

(4) In this section—

"pupil"—

(a) in relation to an Academy school or an alternative provision Academy, means a registered pupil at the Academy;

(b) in relation to a 16 to 19 Academy, means a person receiving education at the Academy;

"relevant pupil", in relation to Academy, means a pupil at the Academy who—

(a) is looked after by a local authority,

(b) was looked after by a local authority but has ceased to be so looked after as a result of a relevant order, or

(c) appears to the proprietor of the Academy—

(i) to have been in state care in a place outside England and Wales because he or she would not otherwise have been cared for adequately, and

(ii) to have ceased to be in that state care as a result of being adopted;

"relevant order" means—

(a) a child arrangements order (within the meaning given by section 8(1) of the Children Act 1989) which includes arrangements relating to—

(i) with whom a child is to live, or

(ii) when a child is to live with any person,

(b) a special guardianship order (within the meaning given by section 14A(1) of the Children Act 1989), or

(c) an adoption order (within the meaning given by section 72(1) of the Adoption Act 1976 or section 46(1) of the Adoption and Children Act 2002).

(5) For the purposes of this section a person is "looked after by a local authority" if the person is looked after by a local authority for the purposes of the Children Act 1989 or Part 6 of the Social Services and Well-being (Wales) Act 2014 (anaw 4).

(6) For the purposes of this section a person is in "state care" if he or she is in the care of, or accommodated by—
  (a) a public authority,
  (b) a religious organisation, or
  (c) any other organisation the sole or main purpose of which is to benefit society.

(7) For the purposes of section 569 of EA 1996 (as applied by section 17(4)), regulations under subsection (3)(b) are to be treated as if the statutory instrument containing them fell within subsection (2A) of that section (regulations subject to affirmative procedure)."

(2) After section 2 of the Academies Act 2010 insert—

"Provision to be included in Academy agreements".

7 Maintained schools: guidance for staff member for looked after pupils

In section 20 of the Children and Young Persons Act 2008 (designated staff member for looked after pupils) after subsection (2) insert—

"(2A) If the school is in England, the governing body must ensure that the designated person has regard to any guidance issued by the Secretary of State."

Care and adoption proceedings in England and Wales

8 Care orders: permanence provisions

In section 31 of the Children Act 1989 (care and supervision orders), for subsection (3B) substitute—

"(3B) For the purposes of subsection (3A), the permanence provisions of a section 31A plan are—
  (a) such of the plan's provisions setting out the long-term plan for the upbringing of the child concerned as provide for any of the following—
    (i) the child to live with any parent of the child's or with any other member of, or any friend of, the child's family;
    (ii) adoption;
    (iii) long-term care not within sub-paragraph (i) or (ii);
  (b) such of the plan's provisions as set out any of the following—

(i) the impact on the child concerned of any harm that he or she suffered or was likely to suffer;
(ii) the current and future needs of the child (including needs arising out of that impact);
(iii) the way in which the long-term plan for the upbringing of the child would meet those current and future needs."

9 Adoption: duty to have regard to relationship with adopters

In section 1(4) of the Adoption and Children Act 2002 (matters to which court is to have regard in coming to a decision relating to the adoption of a child), in paragraph (f) (relationships), after "relatives," in the first place it occurs, insert "with any person who is a prospective adopter with whom the child is placed,".

Secure accommodation

10 Placing children in secure accommodation elsewhere in Great Britain

Schedule 1 contains amendments relating to—
(a) the placement by local authorities in England and Wales of children in secure accommodation in Scotland, and
(b) the placement by local authorities in Scotland of children in secure accommodation in England and Wales.

Chapter 1: consequential amendments

11 Chapter 1: consequential amendments

Schedule 2 contains amendments consequential on this Chapter.

CHAPTER 2

SAFEGUARDING OF CHILDREN

Child Safeguarding Practice Review Panel

12 Child Safeguarding Practice Review Panel

In the Children Act 2004, before section 17 insert—

"Child Safeguarding Practice Review Panel

16A Child Safeguarding Practice Review Panel

(1) The Secretary of State must establish a panel to be known as the Child Safeguarding Practice Review Panel.

(2) The Secretary of State may make any arrangements that the Secretary of State considers appropriate for the establishment of the Panel in accordance with this section.

(3) The Panel is to consist of a chair and members appointed by the Secretary of State.

(4) A person may be appointed for a particular period or otherwise.

(5) The Secretary of State may remove the chair or a member of the Panel if satisfied that the chair or member—
   (a) has become unfit or unable to discharge his or her functions properly, or
   (b) has behaved in a way that is not compatible with continuing in office.

(6) The arrangements that may be made by the Secretary of State under subsection (2) include arrangements about—
   (a) the Panel's proceedings;
   (b) annual or other reports.

(7) The Secretary of State may provide staff, facilities or other assistance to the Panel (and the arrangements that may be made under this section include arrangements about those matters).

(8) The Secretary of State may pay remuneration or expenses to the chair and members of the Panel."

13   Functions of the Panel

In the Children Act 2004, after section 16A (inserted by section 12), insert—

"16B Functions of the Panel

(1) The functions of the Child Safeguarding Practice Review Panel are, in accordance with regulations made by the Secretary of State—
   (a) to identify serious child safeguarding cases in England which raise issues that are complex or of national importance, and
   (b) where they consider it appropriate, to arrange for those cases to be reviewed under their supervision.

(2) The purpose of a review under subsection (1)(b) is to identify any improvements that should be made by safeguarding partners or others to safeguard and promote the welfare of children.

(3) Where the Panel arrange for a case to be reviewed under their supervision, they must—
   (a) ensure that the reviewer provides a report on the outcome of the review;
   (b) ensure—
      (i) that the reviewer makes satisfactory progress, and
      (ii) that the report is of satisfactory quality;
   (c) provide the report to the Secretary of State.

(4) The Panel must publish the report, unless they consider it inappropriate to do so.

(5) If the Panel consider it inappropriate to publish the report, they must publish any information relating to the improvements that should be made following the review that they consider it appropriate to publish.

(6) Regulations under this section may include provision about—
   (a) criteria to be taken into account by the Panel in determining whether serious child safeguarding cases raise issues that are complex or of national importance;
   (b) eligibility for appointment as a reviewer;
   (c) the selection process for appointment of a reviewer;
   (d) the person who is to select a reviewer;
   (e) the supervisory powers of the Panel in relation to a reviewer;
   (f) removal of a reviewer;
   (g) payments of remuneration or expenses to a reviewer by the Secretary of State;
   (h) the procedure for a review;
   (i) the form and content of a report;
   (j) the time when a report is to be provided to the Secretary of State, or published.

(7) The Panel must have regard to any guidance given by the Secretary of State in connection with functions conferred by this section.

(8) Guidance given by the Secretary of State may include guidance about—
   (a) circumstances in which it may be appropriate for a serious child safeguarding case to be reviewed;
   (b) matters to be taken into account in deciding whether a review is making satisfactory progress or whether a report is of satisfactory quality.

(9) In this section—

a "reviewer" means any one or more persons appointed to review a case under the supervision of the Panel;

"safeguarding partners" means persons who, under section 16E, are safeguarding partners in relation to one or more local authority areas in England (see subsection (3) of that section);

"serious child safeguarding cases" means cases in which—
   (a) abuse or neglect of a child is known or suspected by a local authority or another person exercising functions in relation to children, and
   (b) the child has died or been seriously harmed;

"serious harm" includes serious or long-term impairment of mental health or intellectual, emotional, social or behavioural development."

14   Events to be notified to the Panel

In the Children Act 2004, after section 16B (inserted by section 13), insert—

"16C Events to be notified to the Panel

(1) Where a local authority in England knows or suspects that a child has been abused or neglected, the local authority must notify the Child Safeguarding Practice Review Panel if—
   (a) the child dies or is seriously harmed in the local authority's area, or
   (b) while normally resident in the local authority's area, the child dies or is seriously harmed outside England.

(2) A local authority in England must have regard to any guidance given by the Secretary of State in connection with their functions under this section.

(3) In this section "serious harm" has the meaning given by section 16B(9)."

15 Information

In the Children Act 2004, after section 16C (inserted by section 14), insert—

"16D Information

(1) The Child Safeguarding Practice Review Panel may, for the purpose of enabling or assisting the performance of a function conferred by section 16B, request a person or body to provide information specified in the request to—
   (a) the Panel,
   (b) a reviewer, or
   (c) another person or body specified in the request.

(2) The person or body to whom a request under this section is made must comply with the request.

(3) The Panel may enforce the duty under subsection (2) against the person or body by making an application to the High Court or the county court for an injunction.

(4) The information may be used by the Panel, reviewer, or other person or body to whom it is provided only for the purpose mentioned in subsection (1).

(5) In this section "reviewer" means any one or more persons appointed to review a case under the supervision of the Panel."

Local arrangements for safeguarding and promoting welfare of children

16 Local arrangements for safeguarding and promoting welfare of children

After section 16D of the Children Act 2004 (inserted by section 15 of this Act) insert—

"Safeguarding partners for local authority areas

16E Local arrangements for safeguarding and promoting welfare of children

(1) The safeguarding partners for a local authority area in England must make arrangements for—
   (a) the safeguarding partners, and
   (b) any relevant agencies that they consider appropriate,

to work together in exercising their functions, so far as the functions are exercised for the purpose of safeguarding and promoting the welfare of children in the area.

(2) The arrangements must include arrangements for the safeguarding partners to work together to identify and respond to the needs of children in the area.

(3) In this section—

"relevant agency", in relation to a local authority area in England, means a person who—
   (a) is specified in regulations made by the Secretary of State, and
   (b) exercises functions in that area in relation to children;

"safeguarding partner", in relation to a local authority area in England, means—
   (a) the local authority;
   (b) a clinical commissioning group for an area any part of which falls within the local authority area;
   (c) the chief officer of police for a police area any part of which falls within the local authority area."

17 Local child safeguarding practice reviews

After section 16E of the Children Act 2004 (inserted by section 16 of this Act) insert—

"16F Local child safeguarding practice reviews

(1) The safeguarding partners for a local authority area in England must make arrangements in accordance with this section—
   (a) to identify serious child safeguarding cases which raise issues of importance in relation to the area, and
   (b) for those cases to be reviewed under the supervision of the safeguarding partners, where they consider it appropriate.

(2) The purpose of a review under subsection (1)(b) is to identify any improvements that should be made by persons in the area to safeguard and promote the welfare of children.

(3) Where a case is reviewed under the supervision of the safeguarding partners, they must—
   (a) ensure that the reviewer provides a report on the outcome of the review;
   (b) ensure—

(i) that the reviewer makes satisfactory progress, and
(ii) that the report is of satisfactory quality;
(c) provide the report to the Secretary of State and the Child Safeguarding Practice Review Panel.

(4) The safeguarding partners must publish the report, unless they consider it inappropriate to do so.

(5) If the safeguarding partners consider it inappropriate to publish the report, they must publish any information relating to the improvements that should be made following the review that they consider it appropriate to publish.

(6) The Secretary of State may by regulations make provision about—
(a) criteria to be taken into account by the safeguarding partners in determining whether serious child safeguarding cases raise issues of importance in relation to the area;
(b) the appointment or removal of a reviewer by the safeguarding partners, including provision for a reviewer to be appointed by the safeguarding partners from a list provided by the Secretary of State;
(c) the time when a report is to be provided to the Secretary of State or the Child Safeguarding Practice Review Panel, or published;
(d) the procedure for a review;
(e) the form and content of a report.

(7) In this section "reviewer" means any one or more persons appointed to review a case under the supervision of the safeguarding partners for a local authority area."

18 Further provision about arrangements

After section 16F of the Children Act 2004 (inserted by section 17 of this Act) insert—

"16G Further provision about arrangements

(1) This section applies in relation to arrangements made under section 16E or 16F by the safeguarding partners for a local authority area in England.

(2) The safeguarding partners must publish the arrangements.

(3) The arrangements must include arrangements for scrutiny by an independent person of the effectiveness of the arrangements.

(4) The safeguarding partners and relevant agencies for the local authority area must act in accordance with the arrangements.

(5) Subsection (6) applies where a person is specified in regulations under section 16E(3) for the purposes of the definition of "relevant agency".

(6) The regulations may make provision for the enforcement against the person of the duty imposed by subsection (4), if the Secretary of State considers that there would otherwise be no appropriate means of enforcing that duty against the person (but the regulations may not create criminal offences).

(7) At least once in every 12 month period, the safeguarding partners must prepare and publish a report on—
  (a) what the safeguarding partners and relevant agencies for the local authority area have done as a result of the arrangements, and
  (b) how effective the arrangements have been in practice."

19 Information

After section 16G of the Children Act 2004 (inserted by section 18 of this Act) insert—

"16H Information

(1) Any of the safeguarding partners for a local authority area in England may, for the purpose of enabling or assisting the performance of functions conferred by section 16E or 16F, request a person or body to provide information specified in the request to—
  (a) the safeguarding partner or any other safeguarding partner for the area,
  (b) any of the relevant agencies for the area,
  (c) a reviewer, or
  (d) another person or body specified in the request.

(2) The person or body to whom a request under this section is made must comply with the request.

(3) The safeguarding partner that made the request may enforce the duty under subsection (2) against the person or body by making an application to the High Court or the county court for an injunction.

(4) The information may be used by the person or body to whom it is provided only for the purpose mentioned in subsection (1)."

20 Funding

After section 16H of the Children Act 2004 (inserted by section 19 of this Act) insert—

"16I Funding

(1) The safeguarding partners for a local authority area in England may make payments towards expenditure incurred in connection with arrangements under section 16E or 16F—
  (a) by making payments directly, or
  (b) by contributing to a fund out of which the payments may be made.

(2) The payments that may be made include payments of remuneration, allowances or expenses to a reviewer or an independent person.

(3) The safeguarding partners for a local authority area in England may provide staff, goods, services, accommodation or other resources to any person for purposes connected with arrangements under section 16E or 16F.

(4) Relevant agencies for a local authority area in England may make payments towards expenditure incurred in connection with arrangements under section 16E—
   (a) by making payments directly, or
   (b) by contributing to a fund out of which the payments may be made.

(5) In this section an "independent person" means an independent person mentioned in section 16G(3)."

21 Combining safeguarding partner areas and delegating functions

After section 16I of the Children Act 2004 (inserted by section 20 of this Act) insert—

"16J Combining safeguarding partner areas and delegating functions

(1) The safeguarding partners for two or more local authority areas in England may agree that their areas are to be treated as a single area for the purposes of sections 16E to 16I and subsections (3) to (5) of this section.

(2) References in sections 16E to 16I and in subsections (3) to (5) of this section to a local authority area are to be read in accordance with any agreement under subsection (1).

(3) Where a local authority is a safeguarding partner for the same local authority area as another local authority (as a result of an agreement under subsection (1)), the authorities may arrange for one of them to carry out functions under sections 16E to 16I on behalf of the other.

(4) Where a clinical commissioning group is a safeguarding partner for the same local authority area as another clinical commissioning group, the groups may arrange for one of them to carry out functions under sections 16E to 16I on behalf of the other.

(5) Where a chief officer of police is a safeguarding partner for the same area as another chief officer of police, the officers may arrange for one of them to carry out functions under sections 16E to 16I on behalf of the other."

22 Guidance by Secretary of State

After section 16J of the Children Act 2004 (inserted by section 21 of this Act) insert—

"16K Guidance by Secretary of State

(1) The safeguarding partners and relevant agencies for a local authority area in England must have regard to any guidance given by the Secretary of State in connection with functions conferred on them by sections 16E to 16J.

(2) Guidance given by the Secretary of State in connection with functions conferred by section 16F may include guidance about—
   (a) circumstances in which it may be appropriate for a serious child safeguarding case to be reviewed;
   (b) matters to be taken into account in deciding whether a review is making satisfactory progress or whether a report is of satisfactory quality."

23 Interpretation

After section 16K of the Children Act 2004 (inserted by section 22 of this Act) insert—

"16L Interpretation of sections 16E to 16K

In sections 16E to 16K—

"reviewer" has the meaning given by section 16F(7);

"safeguarding partner", in relation to a local authority area, has the meaning given by section 16E(3);

"serious child safeguarding cases" has the meaning given by section 16B(9);

"relevant agency", in relation to a local authority area, has the meaning given by section 16E(3)."

Child death reviews

24 Child death reviews

After section 16L of the Children Act 2004 (inserted by section 23 of this Act) insert—

"Child death review partners for local authority areas

16M Child death reviews

(1) The child death review partners for a local authority area in England must make arrangements for the review of each death of a child normally resident in the area.

(2) The child death review partners may also, if they consider it appropriate, make arrangements for the review of a death in their area of a child not normally resident there.

(3) The child death review partners must make arrangements for the analysis of information about deaths reviewed under this section.

(4) The purposes of a review or analysis under this section are—
   (a) to identify any matters relating to the death or deaths that are relevant to the welfare of children in the area or to public health and safety, and
   (b) to consider whether it would be appropriate for anyone to take action in relation to any matters identified.

(5) Where the child death review partners consider that it would be appropriate for a person to take action as mentioned in subsection (4)(b), they must inform that person.

(6) The child death review partners for a local authority area in England must, at such intervals as they consider appropriate, prepare and publish a report on—
   (a) what they have done as a result of the arrangements under this section, and
   (b) how effective the arrangements have been in practice."

25 Information

After section 16M of the Children Act 2004 (inserted by section 24 of this Act) insert—

"16N Information

(1) Any of the child death review partners for a local authority area in England may, for the purpose of enabling or assisting the performance of functions conferred by section 16M, request a person or body to provide information specified in the request to—
   (a) the child death review partner or any other child death review partner for the area, or
   (b) another person or body.

(2) The person or body to whom a request under this section is made must comply with the request.

(3) The child death review partner that made the request may enforce the duty under subsection (2) against the person or body by making an application to the High Court or the county court for an injunction.

(4) The information may be used by the person or body to whom it is provided only for the purpose mentioned in subsection (1)."

26 Funding

After section 16N of the Children Act 2004 (inserted by section 25 of this Act) insert—

"16O Funding

(1) The child death review partners for a local authority area in England may make payments towards expenditure incurred in connection with arrangements under section 16M—
   (a) by making payments directly, or
   (b) by contributing to a fund out of which payments may be made.

(2) The child death review partners for a local authority area in England may provide staff, goods, services, accommodation or other resources to any person for purposes connected with arrangements under section 16M."

27 Combining child death review partner areas and delegating functions

After section 16O of the Children Act 2004 (inserted by section 26 of this Act) insert—

"16P Combining child death review partner areas and delegating functions

(1) The child death review partners for two or more local authority areas in England may agree that their areas are to be treated as a single area for the purposes of sections 16M to 16O and subsections (3) and (4) of this section.

(2) References in sections 16M to 16O and in subsections (3) and (4) of this section to a local authority area are to be read in accordance with any agreement under subsection (1).

(3) Where a local authority is a child death review partner for the same local authority area as another local authority (as a result of an agreement under subsection (1)), the authorities may arrange for one of them to carry out functions under sections 16M to 16O on behalf of the other.

(4) Where a clinical commissioning group is a child death review partner for the same local authority area as another clinical commissioning group, the groups may arrange for one of them to carry out functions under sections 16M to 16O on behalf of the other."

28 Guidance and interpretation

After section 16P of the Children Act 2004 (inserted by section 27 of this Act) insert—

"16Q Guidance and interpretation

(1) The child death review partners for a local authority area in England must have regard to any guidance given by the Secretary of State in connection with functions conferred on them by sections 16M to 16P.

(2) In this section and sections 16M to 16P "child death review partners", in relation to a local authority area in England, means—
   (a) the local authority;
   (b) any clinical commissioning group for an area any part of which falls within the local authority area."

Miscellaneous

29 Regulations under provisions inserted by sections 13, 16 and 17

In section 66(3) of the Children Act 2004 (regulations subject to affirmative procedure), after "12B(1)(b)" insert ", 16B (whether alone or with regulations under section 16F), 16E(3)".

30 Abolition of Local Safeguarding Children Boards

Omit sections 13 to 16 of the Children Act 2004 (Local Safeguarding Children Boards).

31 Chapter 2: consequential amendments

Schedule 2 contains amendments consequential on this Chapter.

CHAPTER 3

OTHER PROVISION RELATING TO CHILDREN'S SOCIAL CARE

Children's social care: pre-employment protection of whistle-blowers

32   Pre-employment protection of whistle-blowers

(1) Part 5A of the Employment Rights Act 1996 is amended as follows.

(2) In the Part heading omit "in the Health Service".

(3) In section 49B, in the heading, at the beginning insert "The health service:".

(4) After section 49B insert—

> **"49C Children's social care: regulations prohibiting discrimination because of protected disclosure**
>
> (1) The Secretary of State may make regulations prohibiting a relevant employer from discriminating against a person who applies for a children's social care position (an "applicant") because it appears to the employer that the applicant has made a protected disclosure.
>
> (2) A "position" means a position in which a person works under—
> (a) a contract of employment,
> (b) a contract to do work personally, or
> (c) the terms of an appointment to an office or post.
>
> (3) A position is a "children's social care position" if the work done in it relates to the children's social care functions of a relevant employer.
>
> (4) For the purposes of subsection (1), a relevant employer discriminates against an applicant if the employer refuses the applicant's application or in some other way treats the applicant less favourably than it treats or would treat other applicants for the same position.
>
> (5) Regulations under this section may, in particular—
> (a) make provision as to circumstances in which discrimination by a worker or agent of a relevant employer is to be treated, for the purposes of the regulations, as discrimination by the employer;
> (b) confer jurisdiction (including exclusive jurisdiction) on employment tribunals or the Employment Appeal Tribunal;
> (c) make provision for or about the grant or enforcement of specified remedies by a court or tribunal;
> (d) make provision for the making of awards of compensation calculated in accordance with the regulations;
> (e) make different provision for different cases or circumstances;
> (f) make incidental or consequential provision, including incidental or consequential provision amending—
>   (i) an Act of Parliament (including this Act),
>   (ii) an Act of the Scottish Parliament,

(iii) a Measure or Act of the National Assembly for Wales, or
(iv) an instrument made under an Act or Measure within any of sub-paragraphs (i) to (iii).

(6) Subsection (5)(f) does not affect the application of section 236(5) to the power conferred by this section.

(7) "Relevant employer" means any of the following that are prescribed by regulations under this section—
   (a) a local authority in England;
   (b) a body corporate that, under arrangements made by a local authority in England under section 1 of the Children and Young Persons Act 2008, exercises children's social care functions;
   (c) a person who, as a result of a direction under section 497A(4) or (4A) of the Education Act 1996 as applied by section 50 of the Children Act 2004 (local authorities in England: intervention by Secretary of State) exercises children's social care functions;
   (d) the council of a county or county borough in Wales;
   (e) a person who, as a result of a direction under any of sections 153 to 157 of the Social Services and Well-being (Wales) Act 2014, exercises children's social care functions;
   (f) a council constituted under section 2 of the Local Government etc (Scotland) Act 1994.

(8) A "local authority in England" means—
   (a) a county council in England;
   (b) a district council;
   (c) a London borough council;
   (d) the Common Council of the City of London (in their capacity as a local authority);
   (e) the Council of the Isles of Scilly;
   (f) a combined authority established under section 103 of the Local Democracy, Economic Development and Construction Act 2009.

(9) "Children's social care functions"—
   (a) in relation to a relevant employer referred to in subsection (7)(a) to (c), means functions of a local authority in England under—
      (i) any legislation specified in Schedule 1 to the Local Authority Social Services Act 1970 so far as relating to those under the age of 18;
      (ii) sections 23C to 24D of the Children Act 1989, so far as not within sub-paragraph (i);
      (iii) the Children Act 2004;
      (iv) any subordinate legislation (within the meaning given by section 21(1) of the Interpretation Act 1978) under the legislation mentioned in sub-paragraphs (i) to (iii);
   (b) in relation to a relevant employer referred to in subsection (7)(d) or (e), means any functions relating to the social care of children in Wales that are prescribed by regulations under this section;

(c) in relation to a relevant employer referred to in subsection (7)(f), means any functions relating to the social care of children in Scotland that are prescribed by regulations under this section.

(10) The Secretary of State must consult the Welsh Ministers before making regulations under this section in reliance on subsection (7)(d) or (e) or (9)(b).

(11) The Secretary of State must consult the Scottish Ministers before making regulations under this section in reliance on subsection (7)(f) or (9)(c).

(12) For the purposes of subsection (5)(a)—
  (a) "worker" has the extended meaning given by section 43K, and
  (b) a person is a worker of a relevant employer if the relevant employer is an employer in relation to the person within the extended meaning given by that section."

(5) In section 230(6) (interpretation of references to employees, workers etc) for "and 49B(10)" substitute ", 49B(10) and 49C(12)".

(6) In section 236(3) (orders and regulations subject to affirmative procedure) after "49B," insert "49C,".

Combined authority functions relating to children

33 Power to secure proper performance

(1) In section 50 of the Children Act 2004 (powers of the Secretary of State to secure proper performance etc), after subsection (6) insert—

"(7) If any functions of a local authority in England which are specified in subsection (2) are exercisable by a combined authority by virtue of section 105 of the Local Democracy, Economic Development and Construction Act 2009—
  (a) a reference in this section to a local authority includes a reference to the combined authority, and
  (b) a reference in this section to functions specified in subsection (2) is, in relation to the combined authority, to be read as a reference to those functions so far as exercisable by the combined authority."

(2) In section 15 of the Childcare Act 2006 (powers of the Secretary of State to secure proper performance etc), after subsection (6) insert—

"(6A) If any functions of an English local authority under this Part are exercisable by a combined authority by virtue of section 105 of the Local Democracy, Economic Development and Construction Act 2009—
  (a) a reference in any of subsections (3) to (6) to an English local authority includes a reference to the combined authority, and
  (b) a reference in those subsections to functions under this Part is, in relation to the combined authority, to be read as a reference to those functions so far as exercisable by the combined authority."

CHAPTER 4

RELATIONSHIPS, SEX AND PSHE EDUCATION

34 Education relating to relationships and sex

(1) The Secretary of State must by regulations make provision requiring—
   (a) relationships education to be provided to pupils of compulsory school age receiving primary education at schools in England;
   (b) relationships and sex education to be provided (instead of sex education) to pupils receiving secondary education at schools in England.

(2) The regulations must include provision—
   (a) requiring the Secretary of State to give guidance to proprietors of schools in relation to the provision of the education and to review the guidance from time to time;
   (b) requiring proprietors of schools to have regard to the guidance;
   (c) requiring proprietors of schools to make statements of policy in relation to the education to be provided, and to make the statements available to parents or other persons;
   (d) about the circumstances in which a pupil (or a pupil below a specified age) is to be excused from receiving relationships and sex education or specified elements of that education.

(3) The regulations must provide that guidance given by virtue of subsection (2)(a) is to be given with a view to ensuring that when relationships education or relationships and sex education is given—
   (a) the pupils learn about—
      (i) safety in forming and maintaining relationships,
      (ii) the characteristics of healthy relationships, and
      (iii) how relationships may affect physical and mental health and well-being, and
   (b) the education is appropriate having regard to the age and the religious background of the pupils.

(4) The regulations may make further provision in connection with the provision of relationships education, or relationships and sex education.

(5) Before making the regulations, the Secretary of State must consult such persons as the Secretary of State considers appropriate.

(6) The regulations may amend any provision (including provision conferring powers) that is made by or under—
   (a) section 342 of the Education Act 1996;
   (b) Chapter 4 of Part 5 of the Education Act 1996;
   (c) Schedule 1 to the Education Act 1996;
   (d) Part 6 of the Education Act 2002;
   (e) Chapter 1 of Part 4 of the Education and Skills Act 2008;
   (f) the Academies Act 2010.

(7) Any duty to make provision by regulations under subsection (1) may be discharged by making that provision by regulations under another Act, so long as the Secretary

of State consults such persons as the Secretary of State considers appropriate before making the regulations under that Act.

(8) The provision that may be made by regulations under subsection (1) by virtue of section 67 includes, in particular, provision amending, repealing or revoking any provision made by or under any Act or any other instrument or document (whenever passed or made).

(9) Regulations under subsection (1) which amend provision made by or under an Act are subject to the affirmative resolution procedure.

(10) Other regulations under subsection (1) are subject to the negative resolution procedure.

(11) Expressions used in this section, where listed in the left-hand column of the table in section 580 of the Education Act 1996, are to be interpreted in accordance with the provisions of that Act listed in the right-hand column in relation to those expressions.

35 Other personal, social, health and economic education

(1) The Secretary of State may by regulations make provision requiring personal, social, health and economic education (beyond that required by virtue of section 34) to be provided—
   (a) to pupils of compulsory school age receiving primary education at schools in England;
   (b) to pupils receiving secondary education at schools in England.

(2) The regulations may include—
   (a) provision requiring the Secretary of State to give guidance to proprietors of schools in relation to the provision of the education;
   (b) provision requiring proprietors of schools to have regard to that guidance;
   (c) provision requiring proprietors of schools to make statements of policy in relation to the education to be provided, and to make the statements available to parents or other persons;
   (d) further provision in connection with the provision of the education.

(3) Before making the regulations, the Secretary of State must consult such persons as the Secretary of State considers appropriate.

(4) The regulations may amend any provision (including provision conferring powers) that is made by or under—
   (a) section 342 of the Education Act 1996;
   (b) Chapter 4 of Part 5 of the Education Act 1996;
   (c) Schedule 1 to the Education Act 1996;
   (d) Part 6 of the Education Act 2002;
   (e) Chapter 1 of Part 4 of the Education and Skills Act 2008;
   (f) the Academies Act 2010.

(5) The provision that may be made by regulations under subsection (1) by virtue of section 67 includes, in particular, provision amending, repealing or revoking any provision made by or under any Act or any other instrument or document (whenever passed or made).

(6) Regulations under subsection (1) which amend provision made by or under an Act are subject to the affirmative resolution procedure.

(7) Other regulations under subsection (1) are subject to the negative resolution procedure.

(8) Expressions used in this section, where listed in the left-hand column of the table in section 580 of the Education Act 1996, are to be interpreted in accordance with the provisions of that Act listed in the right-hand column in relation to those expressions.

(9) A power to make provision under this section does not limit any power to make provision of the same kind under another Act.

PART 2

SOCIAL WORKERS ETC IN ENGLAND

Social Work England

36 Social Work England

(1) A body corporate called Social Work England is established.

(2) Social Work England is referred to in this Part as "the regulator".

(3) Schedule 3 makes further provision about the regulator.

(4) The Secretary of State may by regulations rename Social Work England.

(5) Regulations under subsection (4) may include consequential amendments to any provision contained in or made under this or any other Act.

37 Over-arching objective

(1) The over-arching objective of the regulator in exercising its functions is the protection of the public.

(2) The pursuit by the regulator of its over-arching objective involves the pursuit of the following objectives—
   (a) to protect, promote and maintain the health, safety and well-being of the public;
   (b) to promote and maintain public confidence in social workers in England;
   (c) to promote and maintain proper professional standards for social workers in England.

38 Advisers

(1) The Secretary of State may by regulations—
   (a) permit or require the regulator to appoint one or more people or panels of people to advise the regulator on matters relating to its functions, and
   (b) make provision about the functions of people or panels so appointed.

(2) The regulations may make further provision in connection with the appointment of a person or panel.

(3) For example, the regulations may make provision about—

(a) payments to be made to those appointed;
(b) staff, facilities or other assistance.

Regulation and improvement

39 Registration

(1) The regulator must keep a register of social workers in England.

(2) The Secretary of State may by regulations require the regulator to keep a register of people who are undertaking education or training in England to become social workers.

(3) The Secretary of State may by regulations—
   (a) authorise the regulator to appoint a member of staff as a registrar;
   (b) make provision about the functions of the registrar;
   (c) make other provision in connection with the keeping of a register.

(4) For example, the regulations may make provision about—
   (a) eligibility for registration or continued registration;
   (b) the combination of the registers mentioned in subsections (1) and (2);
   (c) categories of registration;
   (d) the procedure for dealing with registration applications;
   (e) expiry and renewal of entries;
   (f) the content of the register;
   (g) duties to provide information to the regulator;
   (h) suspension or removal from the register;
   (i) restoration of entries;
   (j) appeals against decisions in connection with registration;
   (k) publication of, or access to, the register or information contained in it;
   (l) the procedure for considering, investigating or determining any matter in connection with the register or registration (including standards of proof);
   (m) evidence in legal proceedings of matters contained in the register (including provision for a certificate to be conclusive proof).

40 Restrictions on practice and protected titles

The Secretary of State may by regulations impose prohibitions or restrictions in connection with—
   (a) the carrying out of social work in England;
   (b) the use, in relation to social work in England, of titles or descriptions specified in the regulations;
   (c) the holding out of a person as qualified to carry out social work in England.

41 Professional standards

(1) The regulator must determine and publish professional standards for social workers in England.

(2) If the regulator is required to keep a register of students, it must determine and publish standards of conduct or ethics for registered students.

(3) Before determining a standard under this section the regulator must—
   (a) consult such persons as the regulator considers appropriate, and
   (b) obtain the Secretary of State's approval of the standard.

(4) The Secretary of State may by regulations make provision about arrangements for assessing whether a person meets a professional standard under subsection (1) relating to proficiency.

(5) If the Secretary of State has made regulations under section 48(1)(a) (transfer to the regulator of functions in connection with approved mental health professionals), the reference in subsection (1) to professional standards for social workers in England includes professional standards relating to their work as approved mental health professionals.

42 Improvement standards

(1) The Secretary of State may—
   (a) determine and publish improvement standards for social workers in England;
   (b) carry out assessments of whether people meet improvement standards under paragraph (a).

(2) The Secretary of State may make arrangements for another person to do any or all of those things (and may make payments to that person).

(3) The Secretary of State must consult such persons as the Secretary of State considers appropriate before determining a standard under subsection (1)(a).

(4) In this section "improvement standard" means a professional standard the attainment of which demonstrates particular expertise or specialisation.

(5) Nothing in this section limits anything in section 41.

43 Education and training

(1) The regulator must, in relation to people who are or who wish to become social workers in England, determine and publish standards of education or training.

(2) Before determining a standard under this section the regulator must—
   (a) consult such persons as the regulator considers appropriate, and
   (b) obtain the Secretary of State's approval of the standard.

(3) The Secretary of State may by regulations make provision for the regulator to operate a scheme for the approval of—
   (a) courses of education or training for people who are or who wish to become social workers in England;
   (b) qualifications for people who are or who wish to become social workers in England.

(4) The regulations may make provision in connection with the approval scheme.

(5) For example, the regulations may make provision about—

(a) the criteria for approval or continued approval;
(b) the procedure for approval or renewal of approval;
(c) duties to provide information to the regulator;
(d) inspections in connection with the approval or continued approval of courses or qualifications (including provision for the appointment of people to carry out inspections);
(e) appeals against decisions in connection with approval;
(f) the publication of the scheme.

(6) The provision that may be made under the regulations about the appointment of people to carry out inspections includes provision about—
(a) payments to be made to those appointed;
(b) staff, facilities or other assistance.

44 Discipline and fitness to practise

(1) The regulator must—
(a) make arrangements for protecting the public from social workers in England whose fitness to practise is impaired, and
(b) make arrangements for taking other disciplinary action against social workers in England.

(2) The Secretary of State may by regulations require the regulator to make arrangements for taking disciplinary action against registered students.

(3) The Secretary of State may by regulations make further provision about—
(a) fitness to practise as a social worker in England,
(b) discipline of social workers in England or registered students, and
(c) the arrangements to be made under subsection (1) or (2).

(4) For example, the regulations may make provision about—
(a) the person by whom decisions about discipline or fitness to practise are to be taken on behalf of the regulator;
(b) the appointment of assessors, examiners or legal or other advisers;
(c) the circumstances in which disciplinary action may be taken or the circumstances in which a person's fitness to practise is impaired;
(d) the procedure for considering, investigating or determining disciplinary matters or fitness to practise (including standard of proof);
(e) powers to obtain information;
(f) temporary measures that may be taken against a person pending the outcome of an investigation;
(g) sanctions;
(h) appeals against decisions;
(i) publication of decisions.

(5) The provision that may be made about persons appointed under the regulations includes provision about—
(a) payments to those persons;
(b) staff, facilities or other assistance.

45 Offences

(1) The Secretary of State may by regulations create offences in connection with—
    (a) registration in a register mentioned in section 39;
    (b) prohibitions or restrictions imposed under section 40 (restrictions on practice and protected titles);
    (c) failing to comply with a requirement to provide documents or other information or to attend and give evidence under regulations under section 39 or 44;
    (d) providing false or misleading information or evidence in response to a requirement under regulations under section 39 or 44.

(2) The regulations—
    (a) must provide for the offences to be triable summarily only, and
    (b) may not provide for the offences to be punishable with imprisonment.

Provision of training

46 Ensuring adequate provision of social work training

(1) The Secretary of State may take such steps as the Secretary of State considers appropriate—
    (a) to ensure that adequate provision is made for social work training, and
    (b) to encourage individuals resident in England to undertake social work training.

(2) The power under subsection (1) may, in particular, be used to provide financial or other assistance (subject to any conditions the Secretary of State thinks are appropriate)—
    (a) for individuals resident in England to undertake social work training;
    (b) for organisations providing social work training.

(3) Functions of the Secretary of State under this section may be exercised by any person, or by employees of any person, authorised to do so by the Secretary of State.

(4) For the purpose of determining—
    (a) the terms and effect of an authorisation under subsection (3), and
    (b) the effect of so much of any contract made between the Secretary of State and the authorised person as relates to the exercise of the function,

Part 2 of the Deregulation and Contracting Out Act 1994 has effect as if the authorisation were given by virtue of an order under section 69 of that Act; and in subsection (3) "employee" has the same meaning as in that Part.

(5) In this section "social work training" means education or training that is suitable for people who are or wish to become social workers in England.

47 Exercise by Special Health Authority of functions under section 46(1)(b)

(1) The Secretary of State may direct a Special Health Authority to exercise functions under section 46(1)(b) so far as relating to the provision of financial or other assistance.

(2) The National Health Service Act 2006 has effect as if—

(a) any direction under subsection (1) were a direction under section 7 of that Act, and
(b) any functions exercisable by the Special Health Authority by virtue of a direction under subsection (1) were exercisable under that section.

(3) Directions under subsection (1)—
   (a) must be given by an instrument in writing, and
   (b) may be varied or revoked by subsequent directions.

Approval of courses in relation to mental health professionals

48   Approval of courses for approved mental health professionals

(1) The Secretary of State may by regulations amend section 114ZA of the Mental Health Act 1983 (approval of courses for approved mental health professionals in England) for the purposes of—
   (a) transferring the functions of the Health and Care Professions Council under that section to the regulator;
   (b) giving the regulator power to charge fees for approving courses under that section.

(2) The regulations may include further provision in connection with the approval of courses or charging of fees by the regulator under that section.

(3) For example, the regulations may—
   (a) authorise the regulator to arrange for another person to exercise functions on the regulator's behalf;
   (b) make provision about the setting of criteria for the approval or continued approval of courses;
   (c) make provision about inspections in connection with the approval or continued approval of courses (including provision for the appointment of people to carry out inspections);
   (d) make provision about the procedure for approval or renewal of approval;
   (e) make provision about duties to provide information;
   (f) make provision about appeals against decisions in connection with approval;
   (g) make provision limiting the regulator's power to approve courses run outside the United Kingdom to those run by institutions approved by the regulator or approved by a person with whom the regulator has made arrangements.

(4) The provision that may be made under the regulations about the appointment of people to carry out inspections includes provision about—
   (a) payments to be made to those appointed;
   (b) staff, facilities or other assistance.

(5) If the regulations give the regulator power to charge fees, section 50(2) to (7) apply for the purposes of this section as they apply for the purposes of that section.

49 Approval of courses for best interests assessors

(1) Paragraph 130 of Schedule A1 to the Mental Capacity Act 2005 (assessments in connection with deprivation of liberty: regulations about selection, and eligibility, of persons to carry out assessments) is amended as follows.

(2) After sub-paragraph (2) insert—

"(2A) In relation to England—
- (a) the provision that the regulations may make in relation to a person's training in connection with best interests assessments includes provision for particular training to be specified by Social Work England or the Secretary of State otherwise than in the regulations;
- (b) the provision that the regulations may make in relation to a person's training in connection with other assessments includes provision for particular training to be specified by the Secretary of State otherwise than in the regulations.

(2B) The regulations may give Social Work England power to charge fees for specifying any training as mentioned in sub-paragraph (2A)(a).

(2C) If the regulations give Social Work England power to charge fees, section 50(2) to (7) of the Children and Social Work Act 2017 apply for the purposes of sub-paragraph (2B) as they apply for the purposes of that section."

(3) In sub-paragraph (3)—
- (a) at the beginning insert "In relation to Wales";
- (b) for "the appropriate authority" substitute "the Welsh Ministers".

(4) Omit sub-paragraph (4).

Fees and grants

50 Fees

(1) The Secretary of State may by regulations confer power on the regulator to charge fees in connection with—
- (a) registration or continued registration in a register mentioned in section 39;
- (b) assessing whether a person meets a professional standard relating to proficiency as mentioned in section 41(4);
- (c) approval or continued approval in accordance with a scheme mentioned in section 43.

(2) The regulator is responsible for setting the level of fees in accordance with any provision made by the regulations.

(3) Before determining the level of any fee the regulator must—
- (a) consult any persons they consider appropriate, and
- (b) obtain the approval of the Secretary of State.

(4) The regulations may authorise fees to be set at a level that exceeds the cost of the things in respect of which they are charged.

(5) But the regulations must require the level of any fees to be set with a view to ensuring that, so far as possible, the regulator's fee income does not exceed its expenses (taking one year with another).

(6) Regulations under this section may include provision about the collection and recovery of fees.

(7) The regulations must require the regulator to pay any fee income to the Secretary of State unless the Secretary of State, with the consent of the Treasury, directs otherwise.

51 Grants

(1) The Secretary of State may make grants to the regulator.

(2) A grant under this section may be made subject to any conditions the Secretary of State thinks are appropriate.

Information and co-operation

52 Information and advice

(1) The regulator may publish or disclose information about any matter relating to its functions or give advice about any matter relating to its functions.

(2) The Secretary of State may by regulations —
   (a) make provision requiring the regulator to publish or disclose information, or give advice, under subsection (1);
   (b) make other provision supplementing subsection (1).

53 Duty to co-operate

(1) The regulator must where appropriate co-operate with the following in the exercise of its functions—
   (a) Social Care Wales,
   (b) the Scottish Social Services Council,
   (c) the Northern Ireland Social Care Council, and
   (d) any other person specified in regulations made by the Secretary of State.

(2) Until section 67(3) of the Regulation and Inspection of Social Care (Wales) Act 2016 (anaw 2) comes fully into force, the reference in subsection (1)(a) to Social Care Wales is to be read as a reference to the Care Council for Wales.

Oversight

54 Information for Secretary of State

The regulator must provide any information that the Secretary of State requests in relation to the exercise of the regulator's functions.

55 Default powers

(1) The Secretary of State may give the regulator a remedial direction if the regulator—
  (a) has defaulted in performing any functions and has not remedied the default, or
  (b) is likely to default in performing any function.

(2) The Secretary of State may by regulations make further provision about remedial directions and their enforcement.

(3) For example, the regulations may make provision about—
  (a) the procedure for determining whether the regulator has defaulted or is likely to default;
  (b) the procedure for giving remedial directions;
  (c) the steps that the Secretary of State may take if the regulator fails to comply with a remedial direction (which may include doing anything that the regulator can do);
  (d) the payment by the regulator of any expenses incurred by the Secretary of State (including expenses incurred in making payments to anyone acting on the Secretary of State's behalf).

56 Oversight by the Professional Standards Authority for Health and Social Care

Schedule 4 contains amendments to give the Professional Standards Authority for Health and Social Care functions to oversee the regulator.

Regulations under Part 2

57 Conferral of functions and sub-delegation

(1) Regulations under this Part may be used to confer functions on the regulator or a Minister of the Crown.

(2) Regulations under this Part may confer discretions on the regulator or a Minister of the Crown.

(3) Regulations under this Part may—
  (a) confer power on the regulator to make rules;
  (b) make provision in connection with the procedure for making those rules (including provision requiring the regulator to obtain the Secretary of State's approval before making rules of a specified description).

(4) The provision that may be made in regulations under this Part by virtue of section 67 includes, in particular, provision amending, repealing or revoking any provision made by or under an Act or any other instrument or document (whenever passed or made).

58 Consultation

(1) Before making regulations under this Part the Secretary of State must carry out a public consultation.

(2) Where the Secretary of State lays a draft of an instrument containing regulations under this Part before Parliament, it must be accompanied by a report by the Secretary of State about the consultation.

(3) The duties imposed by subsections (1) and (2) do not apply to regulations under section 36 (renaming of Social Work England).

(4) The duties imposed by subsections (1) and (2) do not apply where the regulations amend other regulations and, in the opinion of the Secretary of State, they do not make any substantial change.

59 Parliamentary procedure for regulations under Part 2

(1) Regulations under section 36 (renaming of Social Work England) are subject to the negative resolution procedure.

(2) Any other regulations under this Part are subject to the affirmative resolution procedure.

Transfer scheme and consequential amendments

60 Transfer scheme

(1) The Secretary of State may make a scheme for the transfer of property, rights and liabilities from the Health and Care Professions Council (the "old regulator") to Social Work England.

(2) The things that may be transferred under a transfer scheme include—
   (a) property, rights and liabilities that could not otherwise be transferred;
   (b) property acquired, and rights and liabilities arising, after the making of the scheme.

(3) A transfer scheme may make consequential, supplementary, incidental or transitional provision and may—
   (a) create rights, or impose liabilities, in relation to property or rights transferred;
   (b) make provision about the continuing effect of things done by the old regulator in respect of anything transferred;
   (c) make provision about the continuation of things (including legal proceedings) in the process of being done by, on behalf of or in relation to the old regulator in respect of anything transferred;
   (d) make provision for references to the old regulator in an instrument or other document in respect of anything transferred to be treated as references to the transferee;
   (e) make provision for the shared ownership or use of property;
   (f) if the TUPE regulations do not apply in relation to the transfer, make provision which is the same or similar.

(4) A transfer scheme may provide—
   (a) for modification by agreement;
   (b) for modifications to have effect from the date when the original scheme came into effect.

(5) In subsection (3)(f), "TUPE regulations" means the Transfer of Undertakings (Protection of Employment) Regulations 2006 (SI 2006/246).

(6) In this section—

(a) references to rights and liabilities include rights and liabilities relating to a contract of employment;

(b) references to the transfer of property include the grant of a lease.

61 Repeal of existing powers to regulate social workers

(1) The Health Act 1999 is amended as follows.

(2) In section 60 (regulation of health professions, social workers, other care workers etc)—

(a) in subsection (1), omit paragraphs (ba) and (bb);

(b) in subsection (2), in paragraphs (c) and (d), omit "(other than the social work profession in England)";

(c) omit subsection (2ZA);

(d) in subsection (2ZC), omit paragraph (o);

(e) for subsection (2ZE) substitute—

"(2ZEA) In subsection (2ZC) "social work in England" means social work which is required in connection with any health, education or social services provided in England.";

(f) in the heading, for ", social workers, other care" substitute "and social care".

(3) In section 60A (standards of proof in fitness to practise proceedings)—

(a) in subsection (2A), omit paragraph (b);

(b) in subsection (2A)(c), for "that section" substitute "section 60";

(c) in subsection (3), omit "or the social work profession in England (within the meaning given in section 60(2ZA)".

(4) In Schedule 3 (regulation of health care and associated professions)—

(a) in paragraph 10, for the definitions of "social care work in England", "social care workers in England" and "the social work profession in England" substitute—

""social care work in England" and "social care workers in England" have the meaning given by section 60.";

(b) in paragraph 11(2A)(b), for "members of the social work profession in England" substitute "engaging in social work in England".

62 Amendments to do with this Part

Schedule 5 contains further minor and consequential amendments relating to this Part.

Interpretation

63 Interpretation of Part 2

(1) In this Part—

"approved mental health professional" has the meaning given by section 114 of the Mental Health Act 1983;

"Minister of the Crown" has the same meaning as in the Ministers of the Crown Act 1975;

"professional standards" includes standards relating to—
(a) proficiency;
(b) performance;
(c) conduct and ethics;
(d) continuing professional training and development;

"register" means a register mentioned in section 39(1) or (2) (and related expressions are to be read accordingly);

"register of students" means a register mentioned in section 39(2) (and related expressions are to be read accordingly);

"registered student" means a person registered as someone who is undertaking education or training in England to become a social worker;

"the regulator" has the meaning given by section 36;

"social work in England" means social work which is required in connection with any health, education, or social services provided in England;

"social worker in England" means a person who engages in social work in England (but see subsection (2)).

(2) A person who is a member of a profession to which section 60(2) of the Health Act 1999 applies is not to be treated as a social worker in England by reason only of carrying out work as an approved mental health professional.

Review

64 Review by independent person

(1) The Secretary of State must commission an independent person to—
   (a) review the operation of this Part during the review period, and
   (b) send a report to the Secretary of State on the findings of the review.

(2) In carrying out the review the independent person must consult representatives of social workers in England and anyone else that the person considers appropriate.

(3) On receiving the report the Secretary of State must lay it before Parliament.

(4) The Secretary of State must also lay before Parliament a response to the report.

(5) The review period is 5 years beginning with the day on which section 39(1) comes fully into force.

PART 3

GENERAL

65 Power to make transitional provision

The Secretary of State may by regulations make transitional, transitory or saving provision in connection with the coming into force of any provision of this Act.

66 Power to make consequential provision

(1) The Secretary of State may by regulations make provision that is consequential on any provision made by this Act.

(2) Regulations under this section may amend, repeal or revoke any provision made by or under an Act passed before this Act or in the same Session.

(3) Regulations under this section that repeal or amend a provision of an Act are subject to the affirmative resolution procedure.

(4) Any other regulations under this section are subject to the negative resolution procedure.

67 Regulations: general

(1) Regulations under this Act are to be made by statutory instrument.

(2) Regulations under this Act may make—
 (a) consequential, supplementary, incidental, transitional or saving provision;
 (b) different provision for different purposes.

(3) This section does not apply to regulations under section 70.

68 Affirmative and negative resolution procedures

(1) Where regulations under this Act are subject to "the negative resolution procedure" the statutory instrument containing the regulations is subject to annulment in pursuance of a resolution of either House of Parliament.

(2) Where regulations under this Act are subject to "the affirmative resolution procedure" the regulations may not be made unless a draft of the statutory instrument containing them has been laid before Parliament and approved by a resolution of each House of Parliament.

(3) Any provision that may be included in an instrument under this Act subject to the negative resolution procedure may be made by regulations subject to the affirmative resolution procedure.

69 Extent

(1) Section 10 and paragraphs 2, 4, 5 and 14 of Schedule 1 extend to England and Wales and Scotland.

(2) Except as mentioned in subsection (1), any amendment or repeal made by this Act has the same extent as the provision amended or repealed.

(3) Subject to subsections (1) and (2), Parts 1 and 2 extend to England and Wales only.

(4) This Part extends to England and Wales, Scotland and Northern Ireland.

70 Commencement

(1) The following come into force on the day on which this Act is passed—
 (a) section 10 and Schedule 1;

(b) this Part.

(2) The other provisions of this Act come into force on such day as the Secretary of State may by regulations made by statutory instrument appoint.

(3) Different days may be appointed for different purposes.

71 Short title

(1) This Act may be cited as the Children and Social Work Act 2017.

SCHEDULES

SCHEDULE 1 — Section 10

PLACING CHILDREN IN SECURE ACCOMMODATION ELSEWHERE IN GREAT BRITAIN

Children Act 1989

1 The Children Act 1989 is amended as follows.

2 (1) Section 25 (use of accommodation in England for restricting liberty of children looked after by English and Welsh local authorities)—
   (a) is to extend also to Scotland, and
   (b) is amended as follows.

(2) In subsection (1)—
   (a) for "or local authority in Wales" substitute "in England or Wales";
   (b) after "accommodation in England" insert "or Scotland".

(3) In subsection (2)—
   (a) in paragraphs (a)(i) and (ii) and (b), after "secure accommodation in England" insert "or Scotland";
   (b) in paragraph (c), for "or local authorities in Wales" substitute "in England or Wales".

(4) After subsection (5) insert—

"(5A) Where a local authority in England or Wales are authorised under this section to keep a child in secure accommodation in Scotland, the person in charge of the accommodation may restrict the child's liberty to the extent that the person considers appropriate, having regard to the terms of any order made by a court under this section."

(5) In subsection (7)—
   (a) in paragraph (c), after "secure accommodation in England" insert "or Scotland";
   (b) after that paragraph, insert—

   "(d) a child may only be placed in secure accommodation that is of a description specified in the regulations (and the description may in particular be framed by reference to whether the accommodation, or the person providing it, has been approved by the Secretary of State or the Scottish Ministers)."

(6) After subsection (8) insert—

"(8A) Sections 168 and 169(1) to (4) of the Children's Hearings (Scotland) Act 2011 (asp 1) (enforcement and absconding) apply in relation to an order under subsection (4) above as they apply in relation to the orders mentioned in section 168(3) or 169(1)(a) of that Act."

3 In paragraph 19(9) of Schedule 2 (restrictions on arrangements for children to live abroad), after "does not apply" insert "—
   (a) to a local authority placing a child in secure accommodation in Scotland under section 25, or
(b)".

Children (Secure Accommodation) Regulations 1991 (S.I. 1991/1505)

4 The Children (Secure Accommodation) Regulations 1991 (S.I. 1991/1505) are amended as follows.

5 In regulation 1—
   (a) in the heading, for "and commencement" substitute ", commencement and extent";
   (b) the existing text becomes paragraph (1);
   (c) after that paragraph insert—

   "(2) This Regulation and Regulations 10 to 13 extend to England and Wales and Scotland.

   (3) Except as provided by paragraph (2), these Regulations extend to England and Wales."

6 In regulation 2(1) (interpretation), in the definition of "children's home", for the words from "means" to the end, substitute "means—
   (a) a private children's home, a community home or a voluntary home in England, or
   (b) an establishment in Scotland (whether managed by a local authority, a voluntary organisation or any other person) which provides residential accommodation for children for the purposes of the Children's Hearings (Scotland) Act 2011, the Children (Scotland) Act 1995 or the Social Work (Scotland) Act 1968".

7 For regulation 3 substitute—

"3 Approval by Secretary of State of secure accommodation in a children's home

"3 Approval by Secretary of State of secure accommodation in a children's home

(1) Accommodation in a children's home shall not be used as secure accommodation unless —
   (a) in the case of accommodation in England, it has been approved by the Secretary of State for that use;
   (b) in the case of accommodation in Scotland, it is provided by a service which has been approved by the Scottish Ministers under paragraph 6(b) of Schedule 12 to the Public Services Reform (Scotland) Act 2010.

(2) Approval by the Secretary of State under paragraph (1) may be given subject to any terms and conditions that the Secretary of State thinks fit."

8   In regulation 17 (records), in the words before paragraph (a), after "children's home" insert "in England".

Secure Accommodation (Scotland) Regulations 2013 (S.S.I. 2013 No. 205)

9   The Secure Accommodation (Scotland) Regulations 2013 (S.S.I. 2013 No. 205) are amended as follows.

10   In regulation 5 (maximum period in secure accommodation), after paragraph (2) insert—

> "(3) This regulation does not apply in relation to a child placed in secure accommodation in Scotland under section 25 of the Children Act 1989 (which allows accommodation in Scotland to be used for restricting the liberty of children looked after by English and Welsh local authorities)."

11   In regulation 15 (records to be kept by managers of secure accommodation in Scotland), after paragraph (2) insert—

> "(3) The managers must provide the Secretary of State or Welsh Ministers, on request, with copies of any records kept under this regulation that relate to a child placed in secure accommodation under section 25 of the Children Act 1989 (which allows local authorities in England or Wales to place children in secure accommodation in Scotland)."

Children's Hearings (Scotland) Act 2011 (Consequential and Transitional Provisions and Savings) Order 2013 (S.I. 2013 No. 1465)

12   In Article 7 of the Children's Hearings (Scotland) Act 2011 (Consequential and Transitional Provisions and Savings) Order 2013 (S.I. 2013 No. 1465) (compulsory supervision orders and interim compulsory supervision orders), after paragraph (2) insert—

> "(3) Where—
> - (a) a compulsory supervision order or interim compulsory supervision order contains a requirement of the type mentioned in section 83(2)(a) of the 2011 Act and a secure accommodation authorisation (as defined in section 85 of that Act),
> - (b) the place at which the child is required to reside in accordance with the order is a place in England or Wales, and
> - (c) by virtue of a decision to consent to the placement of the child in secure accommodation made under article 16, the child is to be placed in secure accommodation within that place,
>
> the order is authority for the child to be placed and kept in secure accommodation within that place."

Social Services and Well-being (Wales) Act 2014 (anaw 4)

13   In section 124(9) of the Social Services and Well-being (Wales) Act 2014 (anaw 4) (restrictions on arrangements for children to live outside England and Wales), after "does not apply" insert "—
> - (a) to a local authority placing a child in secure accommodation in Scotland under section 25 of the Children Act 1989, or
> - (b)".

Saving for existing powers

14 The amendments made by this Schedule to provisions of subordinate legislation do not affect the power to make further subordinate legislation amending or revoking the amended provisions.

SCHEDULE 2

Sections 11 and 31

PART 1 OF THIS ACT: CONSEQUENTIAL AMENDMENTS

PART 1

AMENDMENT RELATING TO CHAPTER 1

Local offer for care leavers

1 In Schedule 1 to the Local Authority Social Services Act 1970 (social services functions of local authorities), in the table, at the appropriate place insert—

""Children and Social Work Act 2017	
Section 2	Local offer for care leavers."

2 In paragraph 1(2)(a) of Schedule 2 to the Children Act 1989 (information to be published by a local authority), in paragraph (i), for ", 23B to 23D, 24A and 24B" substitute "and 23D".

3 In section 135(1)(e) of the Education and Inspections Act 2006 (functions subject to inspection), for "or the Adoption and Children Act 2002 (c. 38)" substitute ", the Adoption and Children Act 2002 or section 2 of the Children and Social Work Act 2017".

4 In section 30 of the Children and Families Act 2014 (local offer for children and young people who have special educational needs or a disability), for "local offer", in each place it occurs (including the title), substitute "SEN and disability local offer".

Advice and support

5 In paragraph 1(1)(g) of Schedule 3 to the Nationality, Immigration and Asylum Act 2002 (kinds of support for which certain people are ineligible), after "23C," insert "23CZB,".

6 In section 83A(5)(a) of the Apprenticeships, Skills, Children and Learning Act 2009 (apprenticeship offer: application to persons provided with support under Children Act 1989)—
   (a) for "21" substitute "25";
   (b) after "23C" insert "or 23CZB".

PART 2

AMENDMENTS RELATING TO ABOLITION OF LOCAL SAFEGUARDING CHILDREN BOARDS

7   In Schedule 1 to the Local Authority Social Services Act 1970 (social services functions of local authorities), in the entry relating to the Children Act 2004—
    (a) for "13 to 16" substitute "16A to 16Q";
    (b) omit "targets for";
    (c) omit ", and to Local Safeguarding Children Boards".

8   (1) Section 83 of the Children Act 1989 (research and returns of information) is amended as follows.

    (2) In subsection (1), in paragraph (aa), for "of Local Safeguarding Children Boards;" substitute "of—
        (i) the Child Safeguarding Practice Review Panel;
        (ii) safeguarding partners (within the meaning given by section 16E(3) of the Children Act 2004) in relation to local authority areas in England;
        (iii) child death review partners (within the meaning given by section 16Q(2) of the Children Act 2004) in relation to local authority areas in England;".

    (3) In subsection (2) omit paragraph (aa).

    (4) In subsection (3) omit paragraph (c) (and the "and" before it).

9   (1) Section 31 of the Children and Young Persons Act 2008 (supply of information concerning deaths of children) is amended as follows.

    (2) In subsections (2) and (4), for "appropriate Board" substitute "appropriate authority".

    (3) In subsection (5), for "Subsection (6) applies" substitute "Subsections (5A) and (6) apply".

    (4) After subsection (5) insert—

        "(5A) Where the registrar's sub-district is in England, the registrar must, before the end of the required period, secure that the appropriate authority is notified—
            (a) of the issuing of the certificate; and
            (b) of the registrar's belief and the grounds for it."

    (5) In subsection (6)—
        (a) at the beginning insert "Where the registrar's sub-district is in Wales,";
        (b) omit "Local Safeguarding Children Board in England or".

    (6) In subsection (7)(c), for "subsection" substitute "subsections (5A) and".

    (7) After subsection (8) insert—

        "(8A) The child death review partners for each local authority area in England must—
            (a) make arrangements for the receipt by them of notifications under this section; and
            (b) publish those arrangements."

(8) In subsection (9) omit "Each Local Safeguarding Children Board in England and".

(9) Subsection (10) is amended as follows.

(10) In the definition of "the appropriate Board"—
   (a) for "Board" substitute "authority";
   (b) in paragraph (a), for "the Local Safeguarding Children Board in England in whose area" substitute "in relation to a register kept for a sub-district in England, the child death review partners for the local authority area within which";
   (c) in paragraph (b), at the beginning insert "in relation to a register kept for a sub-district in Wales,".

(11) At the appropriate place insert—
   ""child death review partners" has the meaning given by section 16Q(2) of the Children Act 2004;".

(12) Omit the definition of "Local Safeguarding Children Board in England".

SCHEDULE 3

Section 36

SOCIAL WORK ENGLAND

Status

1 (1) The regulator is not to be regarded—
   (a) as a servant or agent of the Crown, or
   (b) as enjoying any status, immunity or privilege of the Crown.

(2) The members and staff of the regulator are not to be regarded as Crown servants.

Members

2 The regulator is to consist of—
   (a) a chair appointed by the Secretary of State, and
   (b) such other members as the Secretary of State may appoint.

Term of office

3 A member holds and vacates office in accordance with the terms of the member's appointment (subject as follows).

4 A member may resign by giving written notice to the Secretary of State.

5 The Secretary of State may by notice in writing remove a member who—
   (a) has without reasonable excuse failed to discharge the functions of his or her office, or
   (b) in the opinion of the Secretary of State is otherwise unable or unfit to carry out his or her duties.

Remuneration and pensions

6 The regulator may pay to the members such remuneration, allowances and expenses as the Secretary of State may decide.

7 If required to do so by the Secretary of State, the regulator must—
   (a) pay such pensions or gratuities to or in respect of any member as the Secretary of State may decide;
   (b) pay such sums as the Secretary of State may decide towards provision for the payment of pensions or gratuities to or in respect of any member.

Staff

8 (1) The regulator must appoint a person to be chief executive, but may only appoint a person who has been approved by the Secretary of State.

(2) The chief executive is an employee of the regulator.

(3) The Secretary of State may appoint the first chief executive.

9 The regulator may appoint other staff.

10 (1) The regulator's staff may be appointed on such terms, including relating to remuneration and pension arrangements, as the regulator may decide.

(2) The regulator must obtain the Secretary of State's approval for any terms relating to remuneration or pension arrangements.

Procedure

11 The regulator may determine its own procedure (including quorum).

12 No proceeding is invalidated by—
   (a) a vacancy in the office of chair, or
   (b) a defect in the appointment of any member.

Delegation

13 (1) The regulator may delegate functions to a committee, sub-committee, member or member of staff.

(2) The functions that may be delegated under sub-paragraph (1)—
   (a) include the power conferred by that sub-paragraph, but
   (b) do not include any power or duty to make rules.

14 (1) The regulator may delegate functions to any other person if—
   (a) the regulator considers that the delegation is likely to lead to an improvement in the exercise of its functions, and
   (b) the person has agreed to the terms of the delegation.

(2) The functions that may be delegated under sub-paragraph (1) do not include—
   (a) the power conferred by that sub-paragraph, or
   (b) any power or duty to make rules.

(3) The terms of a delegation under sub-paragraph (1) may include terms requiring payments by the regulator.

15 (1) A function may be delegated under paragraph 13 or 14—
   (a) wholly or partly;
   (b) generally or only in specified circumstances;
   (c) unconditionally or subject to specified conditions.

(2) A delegation does not prevent the regulator (or the person making the delegation, if different) from exercising the function or making other arrangements for its exercise.

(3) A delegation does not affect any liability or responsibility of the regulator for the exercise of its functions.

Membership of committees and sub-committees

16 (1) A committee or sub-committee of the regulator may include persons who are not members of the regulator.

(2) The regulator may pay such remuneration and allowances as the Secretary of State may determine to any person who—
   (a) is a member of a committee or sub-committee, but
   (b) is not a member or member of staff of the regulator.

Annual reports and accounts

17 As soon as possible after the end of each financial year, the regulator must send the Secretary of State a report on the exercise of its functions during the year.

18 (1) The regulator must keep proper accounts and proper records in relation to the accounts.

(2) The regulator must prepare a statement of accounts for each financial year.

(3) The statement must be in such form as the Secretary of State may direct.

(4) The regulator must send a copy of the statement to —
   (a) the Secretary of State, and
   (b) the Comptroller and Auditor General,
within the time period directed by the Secretary of State.

(5) The Comptroller and Auditor General must—
   (a) examine, certify and report on the statement of accounts, and
   (b) send a copy of the certified statement and of the report to the Secretary of State as soon as possible.

19 The Secretary of State must, in respect of each financial year, lay before Parliament a document consisting of—
   (a) the annual report sent under paragraph 17, and
   (b) the certified statement of accounts and report sent under paragraph 18(5)(b).

20 In paragraphs 17 to 19 "financial year" means—
   (a) the period beginning with the day on which this Schedule comes fully into force and ending with the following 31 March, and
   (b) every subsequent period of 12 months ending with 31 March.

Application of seal and evidence

21 The application of the regulator's seal must be authenticated by the signature of—
   (a) a member of the regulator, or
   (b) any other person who is authorised (generally or specially) for that purpose.

22 A document purporting to be duly executed under the seal of the regulator—
   (a) is to be received in evidence, and
   (b) is to be treated as so executed unless the contrary is shown.

Disqualification

23 In Part 2 of Schedule 1 to the House of Commons Disqualification Act 1975 (bodies of which all members are disqualified), at the appropriate place insert—
   "Social Work England."

Freedom of information

24 In Part 6 of Schedule 1 to the Freedom of Information Act 2000 (other public bodies and offices: general), at the appropriate place insert—
   "Social Work England."

SCHEDULE 4

Section 56

OVERSIGHT BY THE PROFESSIONAL STANDARDS AUTHORITY FOR HEALTH AND SOCIAL CARE

1 The National Health Service Reform and Health Care Professions Act 2002 is amended as follows.

2 (1) Section 25 (the Professional Standards Authority for Health and Social Care) is amended as follows.

   (2) In subsection (3), after paragraph (gb) (but before the "and" at the end) insert—
      "(gc) Social Work England".

   (3) For subsection (3A) substitute—

      "(3A) A reference in an enactment to a body mentioned in subsection (3) is not (unless there is express provision to the contrary) to be read as including—
         (a) a reference to Social Work England, or
         (b) a reference to the Health and Care Professions Council, or a regulatory body within subsection (3)(j), so far as it has functions relating to social care workers in England."

   (4) In subsection (3B) for the definition of "the social work profession in England" and "social care workers in England" substitute—
      ""social care workers in England" has the meaning given in section 60 of the 1999 Act."

3 (1) Section 25A (funding of the Authority) is amended as follows.

   (2) In subsection (1), after "regulatory body" insert ", other than Social Work England,".

(3) At the end of the heading insert "by bodies other than Social Work England".

4   After section 25A insert—

> **"25AA Funding of the Authority by Social Work England**
>
> **"25AA "25AA Funding of the Authority by Social Work England**
>
> (1) The Secretary of State must by regulations require Social Work England to pay the Authority periodic fees of such amount as the Secretary of State determines in respect of such of the Authority's functions in relation to Social Work England as are specified in the regulations.
>
> (2) A reference in this section to the Authority's functions does not include a reference to its functions under section 26A.
>
> (3) The regulations must, in particular, provide for the method of determining the amount of a fee under the regulations.
>
> (4) Before determining the amount of a fee under the regulations, the Secretary of State must request the Authority to make a proposal as to the amount of funding that it considers it requires in order to perform for the period to which the fee would apply such of its functions in relation to Social Work England as are specified in the regulations.
>
> (5) The Authority must—
>   (a) comply with a request under subsection (4), but
>   (b) before doing so, consult Social Work England.
>
> (6) Having received a proposal under subsection (5), the Secretary of State may consult Social Work England.
>
> (7) Having taken into account any representations from Social Work England, the Secretary of State must—
>   (a) make a proposal as to the amount of funding that the Secretary of State considers the Authority requires in order to perform for the period to which the fee would apply such of its functions in relation to Social Work England as are specified in the regulations, and
>   (b) determine in accordance with the method provided for under subsection (3) the amount of the fee that Social Work England would be required to pay.
>
> (8) The Secretary of State must—
>   (a) consult the Authority about the proposal under subsection (7)(a) and the determinations under subsection (7)(b), and
>   (b) consult Social Work England about the determination under subsection (7)(b) of the amount it would be required to pay.
>
> (9) Having taken into account such representations as it receives from consultees, the Secretary of State must—
>   (a) determine the amount of funding that the Authority requires in order to perform for the period to which the fee would apply such of its functions in relation to Social Work England as are specified in the regulations, and

(b) determine in accordance with the method provided for under subsection (3) the amount of the fee that Social Work England is to be required to pay.

(10) Regulations under this section requiring payment of a fee may make provision—
  (a) requiring the fee to be paid within such period as is specified;
  (b) requiring interest at such rate as is specified to be paid if the fee is not paid within the period specified under paragraph (a);
  (c) for the recovery of unpaid fees or interest.

(11) The regulations may enable the Secretary of State to redetermine the amount of a fee provided for under the regulations, on a request by the Authority or Social Work England or on the Secretary of State's own initiative.

(12) Before making regulations under this section, the Secretary of State must consult—
  (a) the Authority,
  (b) Social Work England, and
  (c) such other persons as the Secretary of State considers appropriate."

5 In section 25C (appointments to regulatory bodies), in subsection (7), after "Northern Ireland" insert "or Social Work England".

6 (1) Section 25D (power of regulatory bodies to establish voluntary registers) is amended as follows.

(2) In subsection (1), after "regulatory body" insert "other than Social Work England".

(3) In subsection (2), omit paragraph (b) and the "or" before it.

7 In section 25E (section 25D: interpretation), omit subsections (10) and (11).

8 In section 25F (establishment of voluntary register: impact assessment), in subsection (3)(c), for ", users of social care in England and users of social work services in England" substitute "and users of social care in England".

9 In section 25G (power of the Authority to accredit voluntary registers), after subsection (9) insert—

"(10) In this section "regulatory body" does not include Social Work England."

10 In section 25H (accreditation of voluntary register: impact assessment), in subsection (3)(c), for ", users of social care in England and users of social work services in England" substitute "and users of social care in England".

11 In section 25I (functions of the Authority in relation to accredited voluntary registers), in subsection (1)(a), omit ", users of social work services in England".

12 (1) Section 26A (powers of Secretary of State and devolved administrations) is amended as follows.

(2) In subsection (1D), omit paragraph (b).

(3) For subsection (1E) substitute—

"(1E) In subsection (1D), "unregulated social care worker in England" has the meaning given in section 25E."

13 In section 27 (regulatory bodies and the Authority), in subsection (2), after "regulatory body" insert "other than Social Work England".

14 In section 28 (complaints), in subsection (1), after "regulatory body" insert "other than Social Work England".

15 (1) Section 29 (reference to disciplinary cases by the Authority to court) is amended as follows.

(2) After subsection (2) insert—

"(2A) This section also applies to any steps or decisions which are taken by Social Work England (or any of its committees or officers) in connection with fitness to practise or discipline and which are of a description specified in regulations made by the Secretary of State."

(3) For subsection (5A) substitute—

"(5A) In relation to something that is a relevant decision as a result of subsection (2A), "the relevant court" means the High Court of Justice in England and Wales."

16 (1) Section 38 (regulations and orders) is amended as follows.

(2) In subsection (2), after "other than" insert "regulations under 29(2A) or".

(3) In subsection (3), after "28" insert "or 29(2A)".

SCHEDULE 5

Section 62

Amendments to do with Part 2

Part 1

General amendments

London County Council (General Powers) Act 1920

1 In section 18(e) of the London County Council (General Powers) Act 1920, after "under the Health and Social Work Professions Order 2001" insert "or section 39(1) of the Children and Social Work Act 2017".

Medicines Act 1968

2 In section 58 of the Medicines Act 1968, omit subsection (1ZA).

Video Recordings Act 1984

3 In section 3 of the Video Recordings Act 1984, omit subsection (11A).

London Local Authorities Act 1991

4   In section 4 of the London Local Authorities Act 1991, in paragraph (c) of the definition of "establishment for special treatment", after "under the Health and Social Work Professions Order 2001" insert "or section 39(1) of the Children and Social Work Act 2017".

Value Added Tax Act 1994

5   In Part 2 of Schedule 9 to the Value Added Tax Act 1994, in the Notes to Group 7, omit note (2ZA).

Data Protection Act 1998

6   In section 69(1) of the Data Protection Act 1998, in paragraph (h), omit the words from ", except in so far" to the end.

Care Standards Act 2000

7   The Care Standards Act 2000 is amended as follows.

8   (1) Section 55 is amended as follows.

(2) In subsection (2) as substituted by the Regulation and Inspection of Social Care (Wales) Act 2016, omit paragraph (a).

(3) Until the coming into force of the substitution of subsection (2) by the Regulation and Inspection of Social Care (Wales) Act 2016, the old version has effect as if in paragraph (a) after "social work" there were inserted "in Wales".

(4) In subsection (3) as substituted by the Regulation and Inspection of Social Care (Wales) Act 2016, omit paragraph (k).

9   (1) Section 67 is amended as follows.

(2) Omit subsection (1A).

(3) In subsection (2) as substituted by the Regulation and Inspection of Social Care (Wales) Act 2016—
   (a) omit paragraph (a) (including the "and" at the end), and
   (b) in paragraph (b), omit "other".

(4) Until the coming into force of the substitution of subsection (2) by the Regulation and Inspection of Social Care (Wales) Act 2016, the old version has effect as if the words from "courses", in the first place it occurs, to "social workers" were omitted.

Health and Social Work Professions Order 2001

10   The Health and Social Work Professions Order 2001 (SI 2002/254) is amended as follows.

11   (1) Article 3 is amended as follows.

(2) In paragraph (5)(b)—
   (a) in paragraph (ii), after "registrants or" insert "other";
   (b) at end of paragraph (iv) insert "and";

(c) omit paragraphs (vi) and (vii).

(3) Omit paragraph (5AA).

12 In article 6(3)(aa), omit "or social work".

13 In article 7(4), omit "or social work".

14 (1) Article 9 is amended as follows.

(2) Omit paragraph (3A).

(3) In paragraph (8), omit "or social work".

15 (1) Article 10 is amended as follows.

(2) In paragraph (6), omit "or social work".

(3) Omit paragraph (7).

16 In article 11A, omit paragraph (11).

17 (1) Article 12 is amended as follows.

(2) In paragraph (1)—
   (a) at the end of sub-paragraph (b) insert "or";
   (b) omit sub-paragraph (d) and the "or" before it.

(3) In paragraph (2)—
   (a) at the end of sub-paragraph (a) insert "and";
   (b) omit sub-paragraph (c) and the "and" before it.

18 (1) Article 13 is amended as follows.

(2) In paragraph (1), omit "or (1B)".

(3) Omit paragraph (1B).

19 For the heading of article 13A substitute "Visiting health professionals from relevant European States".

20 Omit article 13B.

21 In article 19(2A)(b), omit "or social work".

22 In article 20, omit the words from "; but the reference" to the end.

23 (1) Article 37 is amended as follows.

(2) In paragraph (1)(aa), omit "or social work".

(3) Omit paragraph (1B).

(4) In paragraph (5A)(a), omit the words from "or registered as a social worker" to the end of that sub-paragraph.

(5) In paragraph (8), omit "(other than a hearing on an appeal relating to a social worker in England)".

(6) Omit paragraph (8A).

24 (1) Article 38 is amended as follows.

(2) Omit paragraph (1ZA).

(3) In paragraph (4), omit "(subject to paragraph (5))".

(4) Omit paragraph (5).

25 In article 39, omit paragraph (1A).

26 In Schedule 1, in paragraph 1A(1)(b), omit paragraph (ia) (but not the "and" at the end).

27 (1) In Schedule 3, paragraph 1 is amended as follows.

(2) In the definition of "visiting health or social work professional from a relevant European state", omit "or social work" in both places.

(3) In the definition of "relevant professions", omit "social workers in England;".

(4) Omit the definition of "social worker in England".

Adoption and Children Act 2002

28 (1) In section 10 of the Adoption and Children Act 2002, in subsection (2), for ", one of the registers maintained under" substitute "—
  (a) the register of social workers in England maintained under section 39 of the Children and Social Work Act 2017,
  (b) any register of social care workers in England maintained under an Order in Council under section 60 of the Health Act 1999 or any register maintained under such an Order in Council so far as relating to social care workers in England, or
  (c) the register maintained under"."

(2) Until the coming into force of the amendment made by sub-paragraph (1), section 10(2) of the Adoption and Children Act 2002 is to have effect as if the reference to the registers mentioned there included a reference to the part of the register maintained under article 5 of the Health and Social Work Professions Order 2001 that relates to social workers in England.

Income Tax (Earnings and Pensions) Act 2003

29 In section 343(2) of the Income Tax (Earning and Pensions) Act 2003, in paragraph 1 of the Table, after sub-paragraph (r) insert—
  "(s) the register of social workers in England kept under section 39(1) of the Children and Social Work Act 2017."

National Health Service Act 2006

30 In section 126 of the National Health Service Act 2006, for subsection (4A) substitute—

"(4A) Subsection (4)(h) does not apply to persons in so far as they are registered as social care workers in England (within the meaning of section 60 of the Health Act 1999)."

National Health Service (Wales) Act 2006

31   In section 80 of the National Health Service (Wales) Act 2006, for subsection (4A) substitute—

"(4A) Subsection (4)(h) does not apply to persons in so far as they are registered as social care workers in England (within the meaning of section 60 of the Health Act 1999)."

Armed Forces Act 2006

32   In section 257(3) of the Armed Forces Act 2006, for paragraph (a) substitute—
          "(a)   Social Work England;".

Safeguarding Vulnerable Groups Act 2006

33   The Safeguarding Vulnerable Groups Act 2006 is amended as follows.

34   In section 41(7), in the table, after entry 10 insert—

""11 The register of social workers in England kept under section 39(1) of the Children and Social Work Act 2017	The registrar appointed under section 39(3)(a) of the Children and Social Work Act 2017 or, in the absence of such an appointment, Social Work England"."

35   In Schedule 3, in paragraph 16(4), after paragraph (l) insert—
          "(m)   Social Work England."

Protection of Vulnerable Groups (Scotland) Act 2007 (asp 14)

36   In section 30A(6) of the Protection of Vulnerable Groups (Scotland) Act 2007—
          (a)   omit "the social work profession in England or";
          (b)   for "each of those expressions having the same meaning as in" substitute "within the meaning of".

Children and Young Persons Act 2008

37   (1) In section 2 of the Children and Young Persons Act 2008, in subsection (6), for paragraph (a) substitute—
          "(a)   in the register maintained by Social Work England under section 39(1) of the Children and Social Work Act 2017;".

          (2) Until the coming into force of the amendment made by sub-paragraph (1), section 2(6)(a) of the Children and Young Persons Act 2008 is to have effect as if the reference to the register mentioned there were to a register maintained under article 5 of the Health and Social Work Professions Order 2001.

Health and Social Care Act 2012

38   In the Health and Social Care Act 2012 omit sections 213, 215 and 216.

Regulation and Inspection of Social Care (Wales) Act 2016 (anaw 2)

39 The Regulation and Inspection of Social Care (Wales) Act 2016 is amended as follows.

40 In section 111(4)(b)—
   (a) in the Welsh text, for "Cyngor y Proffesiynau Iechyd a Gofal" substitute "Gwaith Cymdeithasol Lloegr";
   (b) in the English text, for "the Health and Care Professions Council" substitute "Social Work England".

41 In section 117(4)(a)—
   (a) in the Welsh text, after "Gofal" insert "neu Waith Cymdeithasol Lloegr";
   (b) in the English text, after "Council" insert "or Social Work England".

42 In section 119(4)(a)(ii)—
   (a) in the Welsh text, for "y Cyngor Proffesiynau Iechyd a Gofal" substitute "Gwaith Cymdeithasol Lloegr";
   (b) in the English text, for "the Health and Care Professions Council" substitute "Social Work England".

43 In section 125(5)(a)(ii)—
   (a) in the Welsh text, for "y Cyngor Proffesiynau Iechyd a Gofal" substitute "Gwaith Cymdeithasol Lloegr";
   (b) in the English text, for "the Health and Care Professions Council" substitute "Social Work England".

44 In section 174(5)(a)(ii)—
   (a) in the Welsh text, for "Cyngor y Proffesiynau Iechyd a Gofal" substitute "Gwaith Cymdeithasol Lloegr";
   (b) in the English text, for "the Health and Care Professions Council" substitute "Social Work England".

PART 2

RENAMING OF HEALTH AND SOCIAL WORK PROFESSIONS ORDER 2001

45 For the title to the Health and Social Work Professions Order 2001 (SI 2002/254) substitute "Health Professions Order 2001".

46 In article 1(1) of that Order (citation), for "the Health and Social Work Professions Order 2001" substitute "the Health Professions Order 2001".

47 In the following provisions, for "the Health and Social Work Professions Order 2001" substitute "the Health Professions Order 2001"—
   (a) section 18(e) of the London County Council (General Powers) Act 1920;
   (b) section 3(11) of the Video Recordings Act 1984;
   (c) 114ZA(4) of the Mental Health Act 1983;
   (d) paragraph (E) in the entry for the London County Council (General Powers) Act 1920 in Schedule 2 to the Greater London Council (General Powers) Act 1984;
   (e) paragraph (c) of the definition of "establishment for special treatment" in section 4 of the London Local Authorities Act 1991;

(f) item 1(c) in Group 7, in Part 2 of Schedule 9 to the Value Added Tax Act 1994;
(g) section 69(1)(h) of the Data Protection Act 1998;
(h) section 60(2)(c) of the Health Act 1999;
(i) sections 25C(8)(h) and 29(1)(j) of the National Health Service Reform and Health Care Professions Act 2002;
(j) section 126(4)(a) of the National Health Service Act 2006;
(k) section 80(4)(a) of the National Health Service (Wales) Act 2006;
(l) entry 10 in the table in section 41(7) of the Safeguarding Vulnerable Groups Act 2006.

48 In the definition of "registered psychologist" in each of the following provisions, for "the Health and Social Work Professions Order 2001" substitute "the Health Professions Order 2001"—
(a) section 307(1) of the Criminal Procedure (Scotland) Act 1995;
(b) section 207(6) of the Criminal Justice Act 2003;
(c) section 21(2)(b) of the Criminal Justice (Scotland) Act 2003;
(d) section 25 of the Gender Recognition Act 2004.

Adapted and published by GRANGIS under the OGL Licence 3.0.

www.nationalarchives.gov.uk/doc/open-government-licence/version/3/

GRANGIS - UK PUBLISHING 2022.

Thank you for taking the time to leave us a review regarding this version

For further inquiries, contact us at:
www.grangis.com / contact@grangis.com

Printed in Great Britain
by Amazon